FINANCIAL DISTORTION DYNAMICS

Dedicated to my family for their patience, once again

TABLE OF CONTENTS

Introduction... 1
Foundations and Summary of Book Structure
Qualifications and Shortcomings

Part I. Interest Rate Theory: Historical Overview... 4
Terminology
Classical and Modern Approaches... 5
The Classical Interest Rate and Gap... 6
    1. Normal Loan Rate
    2. Natural Rate of Interest (NRI)... 7
    Distinction: Bank Loan Rate, Normal Loan Rate
    Convergence: Natural Closing of the Interest Rate Gap
    Consequences of Interest Rate Gaps... 8
    Discounting and Asset Price Inflation
    Deteriorating Returns and Stagnation
    CHART: *Riskfree* rate (1982-2017)
The Modern Interest Rate Gap and Neutrality... 10
    Neutral Interest Rate and Gap
Reflections... 12
Distortive Causes and Impacts
Logical Circularity
Interest Rates as Infinite

Part II. A Microeconomic Approach to Interest Rate Determination... 13
TABLE: Theories of Interest Rate Determination
(A) Credit-Based Interest Rates, Firm-Specific (Static Cases)
(A.1) Credit-Based Interest Rates (CBI): Existing Debt Loads
Sample Computation of CBI: Static Case

10-Year Term Loan, Matching Amortization, DSC=1.5x
TABLE: CBI (Existing Debt Load) Computation Review
      1. Source of Repayment (SOR)... 17
      2. Principal (P)
      3. Principal/Source of Repayment Multiple (P/SOR)
      CHART: CBIs at Various. P/SOR Multiples
      CBI in 3-Dimensional Format (P/SOR=4)
      CHART: Principal/SOR=4 Example
      4. Interest (CBI): Computed... 20
      CBI with Fitted Exponential Formula
      5. Debt Service Amount (Annual)... 21
      TABLE: Debt service breakdown
      6. Debt Service Coverage Ratio (DSC): Computed

(A.2) Credit-Based, Natural Interest Rates (CNRI): Static Case... 22
Element 1. Debt Service Capacity (DSC)... 23
      CNRI Loan Qualification Example (Static Case)
      The CNRI Schedule
      CHART: CNRI Schedule
            Discrete vs. Continuous
            Interest Rate and Economization
      The CNRI Table and Computation Review... 25
            TABLE: CNRI Computation Review
            Fitted Exponential Curve
            CHART: Actual vs. Fitted Values
      Debt Service Ratio Check... 28
      Adjusting Quantity of Credit
Element 2. Natural Rates of Return

CNRI Determination: Constraints... 30
1. Upper Limit (Borrower): Natural Rate of Return (NRR)
Additional Points for Clarification
Return=Cost
IRR vs. RRC
Real vs. Nominal Interest Rates

Assigning a Value to RRC
Theoretical Upper Limit
CHART: Relative Frequency Distribution RRC
2. Lower Limit/Floor (Lender): Opportunity Cost (of Capital)
Adjusting the Quantity of Credit and Interest Rate: Example
TABLE: CNRI Table Adjusting Quantity of Credit and Int. Rate.
3. Negotiations/Wrap-Up between Lender and Borrower
Closing Comments

(B) Undistorted Credit and Other Markets... 37
Markets vs. Undistorted Markets
Debt-Independent Growth Dynamic
Debt-Income Confusion

Part III. Preliminary Results of Analysis... 39
A. Estimation of CNRI with Historical Data
10-Year Sets, Sequential
Probability Scenarios... 40
TABLE: RRC Probability Scenarios: Left, Right, Center
CNRI Range
CHART: CNRI Range for RRC at P=0.10, $P(X<X_1)$
Fitted Distributions for RRC... 42
Radar Charts
Relative Frequency of Distributions
        TABLE: Top 3

The CNRI and Accounting for Estimation Error... 44
Credit-based Natural Interest Rates:
Estimates vs. 10-Year Bond Rates
CNRI Scenario #1: Left Tail [P=0.05, $P(X<X_1)$]
CNRI Scenario #2: Left Tail [P=0.10, $P(X<X_1)$]
CNRI Scenario #3: Center [P=0.50, $P(X<X_1)$ or $P(X>X_1)$].

B. Evidence of Financial Distortion: Asset Mispricing... 49
B.1. Asset Mispricing: Debt
CHART Debt Accumulation History

CHART Credit-Based Interest Rate (CBI) Estimates
B.2. Asset Mispricing: Equities... 51
Stock Price and Rates of Return (RRC)
Regression Analysis
Relative Frequency Distributions... 53
    CHART: SPG
    CHART: RRCG
    CHARTS: Other Variables (EI%, RRC, REVG)
Ratio Analysis of Fitted Distributions for Selected Probabilities (Radar Charts)... 55
Variables and Methodology
Fitted Distributions
Probabilities and Corresponding Data Points
Valuation and Evidence of Mispricing... 56
Assumptions
Variables and (Over/Under)valuation Ratio
Fundamentals
Subdividing the Distribution
Abbreviations
Summary Findings in Tables... 58
Right Tail Scenario
    TABLE: Right Tail scenario
Left Tail Scenario
    TABLE: Left Tail Scenario
Center Scenario
    TABLE: Center Scenario
    Special Note: Outliers
Summary of Overall Valuation Results... 60
    TABLE: Valuation Summary
Fitted Distributions
Summary Findings in Radar Charts... 61
    Theoretical "Perfect" Valuation Scenario
    CHART: Alignment, Ratio=1 for all sets.
    Notes on Outliers
        TABLE: Right tail Set 12, unadjusted
        Detail

Adjusting for Outliers and Caveats
Scenarios and Interpretation... 64
Right Tail Scenario
    CHART
Left Tail Scenario
    CHART
Center Scenario
    CHART
Summary of Valuation and Mispricing Results... 66
TABLE: Valuations (All scenarios, all sets)
Interpretation of Results

Divergence Viewed in Time Series... 68
CHART: CAGR Changes
CHART: Year over Year (YOY) Changes
Interpretation

Dual Decline Events: REVG and EI%... 71

C. Financial Distortion in Equity Financing: Recognition of Taxpayer Ownership.
Low-Cost Financing Source
Recoupling
Polarity Reversal
Flow-to-Asset Conversion Loop
Summary
Recoupling Accounting Methodology... 74
Example: Contracts and Contract Revenues to Firms
        Journal Entries

APPENDICES

Appendix 1. Distribution Fitting... 76
Introduction and Shortcomings
Distribution Fitting
Data

Variables
Datasets
Description of Datasets
1. **Entire Sample of Each Variable: 5 Datasets... 78**
2. **10-Year Subsamples: 99 Datasets**
Goodness-of-Fit Testing
Results
1. **Entire Sample of Each Variable: 5 Datasets... 80**
Comparing Test Results
EI% and CHART (pdf)
RRC and CHART (pdf)
RRCG and CHART (pdf)
SPG and CHART (pdf)
REVG and CHART (pdf)
Normality
2. **All Datasets (104)... 84**
Relative Frequency
Distribution Types of All Datasets
All Datasets in Radar Charts
CHART: EI%
CHART: RRC
CHART: RRCG
CHART: SPG
CHART: REVG
Regime Changes Among 10-Year Sets... 90
Uniformity: Entire Sample and Subsamples
Initial Best Fit
        TABLE
Alternative Best Fit
        TABLE
Tentative Results... 92
10-Year Sets
Entire Sample
Functions, Parameters and Domains

Appendix 2. Fundamentals and Pricing... 95

Price, Value and Pricing/Valuation
Worthlessness and Value
Mispricing and Valuation
Quantity
Price Interventions
Distortions and Rigged Markets
Fundamentals: Examples... 100
Earnings
Dividends
Revenues
Balance Sheet Measures
Debt and Debt Serviceability
User engagement
Cash Flow
Qualitative/Unobservable Factors
Network effects/Other (Re: Crypto-Assets)
Profit/Net Surplus
Factors Underlying Supply and Demand
        Notes/Detail
                Price Decline Scenarios
Other
Time Frame
Causality and Correlation
Focus on Select Fundamentals... 107
1. Dividends
2. Earnings (Earnings-based Valuation)... 108
Defining earnings fundamentals
3. Rates of Return... 109
EPR: Clarification
Firm-Specific Approach... 110
        Overview: Rate of Return on Cost (RRC)
        RRC as a Fundamental Variable
        Real vs. Nominal
        Financial and Economic Entities Concept
        Natural Rate of Return
        Detail: Equity Income (NNCF)

EI and Dividends
EI and Debt Service (SOR)
   TABLE: Credit-Based Interes
Earnings vs. Equity Income
Revenue Growth and Equity Income
Internal Rate of Return (IRR)... 114
Comparing Fundamental Variables... 115
TABLE: Descriptive Statistics
Regression Estimates

Appendix 3. Relative Frequency Distributions:
A Dynamic View... 118
Static and Dynamic Approaches... 119
Sets 1-16: EI, RRC, RRCG, SPG, REVG

Appendix 4. Policy and System Dynamics Overview... 152
TABLE (part 1 and 2): Subsystem 3

Addendum... 156

REFERENCES... 158
Additional Notes, Resources, and Acknowledgements

INTRODUCTION

The world is awash in debt, of which nearly U.S. $10 trillion is negative-yielding. (Reuters, 2017) Financial crises and systemic risk loom over the economic landscape on a global scale. How did this happen and is there a path to a more sustainable future?

A central thesis of this work is that sustainable credit and economic growth rely upon undistorted interest rates. Traditional approaches to stimulate growth through policy-directed low-cost borrowing have led to debt-fueled, inflationary distortion dynamics. This poses risks of asset bubbles, * financial and banking crises, * unjust wealth transfer, impoverishment through declining real purchasing power and financial repression on savers. Ultimately, the debt burden coupled with income disruption could threaten millions who depend on an unsustainable system.

A microeconomic approach to interest rate determination is examined here: Credit-based natural rates of interest (CNRI). These rates are established in loanable funds markets and reflect adequate debt service capacity based on the underlying natural rates of return (NRR) of individual firms (*firm-specific*). Firm-specific natural rates of interest reflecting natural returns are viewed as key drivers of *self-regulating, sustainable* debt and economic growth, rather than policy interest rates and inflation as vehicles to direct and service debt, respectively.

Other topics featured are a historical overview of interest rate theory; an analysis of financial distortions in debt and equity mispricing; a novel accounting method to address artificially low financing costs for firms that benefit from taxpayer funds due to non-recognition of ownership; a distribution fitting exercise; fundamentals and pricing (with notes on dynamics in the crypto-asset space); and a review of policy interventions in the monetary realm. The analyses employ some three decades of financial data of a global firm in the consumer goods sector with a market capitalization of an estimated U.S. $200 billion as of 2017.

*Notes: 1. E.g. Bubbles in bonds, stocks, real estate, art, and in crypto. (Holland 2017; McCormick and Renick 2017; Reuters 2017; Russo 2017). 2. Policymakers intending to normalize rates are now faced with a "debt trap": Low rates encourage debt while raising rates may trigger massive defaults and losses on bonds (Borio and Disyatat 2014; Juselius, Borio, Disyatat, Drehmann 2017).

Foundations and Summary of Book Structure. The book is divided into three major parts which include the Appendices. Part I provides an overview of theory of interest rates and their determination from a historical perspective; Part II (A) details a microeconomic approach to interest rate determination—*credit-based interest rates, firm-specific*—which begins with review of *credit-based interest rates* (CBI) initially presented in Kennedy (2015) and which are limited to *existing debt loads*; the analysis of interest rate determination is expanded here to *credit-based natural rates of interest* (CNRI) which incorporate *debt service capacity* and *natural rates of return* (NRR) to determine the interest rate that corresponds to a *qualifying* loan amount based on debt service requirements of the lender. Ultimately, natural rates of return are viewed as a fundamental driver not only of value but of sustainable credit and economic growth.

Part II (B) briefly attempts to describe credit markets that are absent of financial distortion, a condition that does not currently exist and may remain only theoretical in many cases. The topic of distortions (Kennedy 2017) is revisited briefly in Appendix 4. References that highlight debt issues and market distortions include BIS 2015, 2017; Grant 1996, 2008, McCormick 2017; Takeo, et al. 2017)

Part III presents a case study and results of an analysis of historical data of a global firm in the consumer goods sector. In Part III (A), the CNRI is estimated while accounting for estimation *error*. Any tentative conclusions are not intended as a guide for policy, only as a potentially informative reference for interest rate determination in the absence of policy rates.

Part III (B) turns to evidence of financial distortion in debt and equities: Historical debt accumulation, and debt mispricing; and equity mispricing based on various analyses including regression, comparison of relative frequency distributions, ratio analysis based on fitted probability distributions, visualization through time series, and dual declines (of revenues and equity income in the same fiscal year). Part III (C) examines financial distortions in the cost of financing for firms receiving taxpayer funds without ownership recognition and suggests a possible accounting methodology.

The appendices provide background details on distribution fitting (Appendix 1), the concept of "fundamentals" and pricing (Appendix 2), and reviews distortions within the financial and monetary realm originally outlined in Kennedy (2017) (Appendix 4). Appendix 3 lays out the relative frequency distributions of the 10-year sets sequentially to provide a dynamic view of the variables studied in a "flip book" format.

Qualifications and Shortcomings. This document first was intended for self-reference while expanding upon previous research and further analyzing interest rate determination in a decentralized context. Shortcomings of the studies are noted wherever possible in the text and appendices, although these are not exhaustive. Exploring solutions to complex problems can lead to the need for specialized fields that professionals are best-equipped to investigate (Cirillo, Fontanari and Taleb 2017; Cook 2008, 2017; Taleb 2017; Re: *explosive uncertainty*; *fat tails*). Therefore, this research might be viewed at best as an incomplete sketch of an intended problem-solving exercise. Despite these failings, as well as typos and errors, omissions and oversights, misinterpretations, contradictions, oversimplifications, unconventional approaches and writing style, it is hoped that some

3

elements of this work might provide some insights towards reducing financial distortions and their potentially devastating consequences. It is crucial to add that any conclusions drawn, including from the estimation of natural interest rates in Part III, does not imply that it would be advisable for policy to attempt to apply such approaches; on the contrary, the likely implication would be the *removal* of policy interventions to allow undistorted credit/loanable funds market to function. That said, at some point should there be policy-guided transition towards undistorted markets, management of the *existing/outstanding debts* would be a major undertaking involving some form of large-scale and long-term restructuring until the debts are fully amortized.

Technical parts familiar to readers can be skipped over or corrected. The reader is encouraged to consult other resources on individual topics to supplement an understanding of the material presented here; terms in *italics* and the abbreviation "Re:" are added to highlight some of the relevant terminology. Conventions adopted in the book and other notes are found in an Addendum before the References.

PART I. Interest Rate Theory: Historical Overview
Terminology

The **stated interest rate** is typically that which is stated on the loan document as a percentage of the amount lent. The **bank loan rate** is computed according to a bank formula to ensure bank profitability. The *cost of funds* to the bank is related closely to monetary policy and policy interest rates (see below).

Yield or Bond Rates. The word "yield" is often confused with the interest rate on a bank loan. Yield is a rate of return measure called the yield-to-maturity (YTM). The YTM is the internal rate of return (IRR) for a stream of cash flow payments based on the initial cost of the bond. The term "yield" is primarily used in a debt market context (e.g. traded debt instruments such as bonds, mortgage-backed security (MBS), etc.). Yields on such instruments may fluctuate considerably and are influenced by policy or "official" interest rates (see below).

4

It is also crucial to note that because of an inverse relationship between yields and the price of debt instruments such as bonds, lower yields translate into higher bond values. This is particularly relevant in the discussion on asset price inflation and debt mispricing, where bond values rise (based on policy interest rates—see just below) along with declining yields, but the values do not reflect underlying *fundamentals*; the topic of fundamentals is addressed in Part II – defined as natural rates of return – as well as in Appendix 2.

Policy Interest rates (official rates) are set typically by monetary authorities/central banks according to policy priorities (e.g. aid in price stability and economic/job growth). For example, in the U.S., the *federal funds rate* and the *interest rate on excess reserves* are set by policy. Monetary policy may also refer to their estimates of the *natural* or *neutral* interest rate both as guides* to setting policy rates, to be detailed further below.

*A distinction will be made here regarding *natural* and *neutral* rates of interest: Natural interest rates should be viewed as primarily linked to the *real* economy/production and *real* rates of return *without* reference to policy interest rates (although monetary policymakers may attempt to estimate them); neutral interest rates are referred to as such primarily in the context of policy interest rates having a less disruptive impact on the structure of production and the economy.

Classical and Modern Approaches

The *natural interest rate* (NRI) or *real interest rate* are different terms to describe essentially the same concept, originating with in the 19th century with Knut Wicksell (1898). Wicksell's work will be referred to as forming part of the classical approach* to interest rate theory that relates *profit* or *rates of profit* to interest rates (also see Locke 1668, Cantillon 1755, Smith 1776, Ricardo 1826). Ricardo provides a good cursory description of this classical view: "The rate of interest, though ultimately and permanently governed by the rate of profit, is however subject to temporary variations from other causes." (Ricardo: 297)

Key Distinction between Rival Classical Views. It is recognized that the renowned economist Irving Fisher (1907, 1930; Re: Fisher's equation and Fisher's law) has also been associated with formulating a classical theory of interest and has been described as the "father" of the theory of interest rates (Brealey and Myers 1996:642, Fabozzi and Modigliani 1992: 336). **Fisher Equation:** Fisher's formulation of the *real interest rate* as the nominal interest rate less the inflation rate, is a fundamental departure from the previous theory.

The Fisher approach to interest rate determination is not viewed here as the "original" classical approach, but rather, to a more *modern* view due to its key departure from the concept of a fundamental link between the rate of profit (returns) and the real interest rate. In the Fisher framework, *interest rate gaps* (see below) in the prior classical sense also cease to exist. The possible 20th-century debt-oriented policy reasons for this shift are conjectured in Kennedy (2016: 124-127).

The Classical Interest Rate and Gap

To understand the development of the ideas more clearly surrounding interest rate theory, it is considered crucial to clarify the components and nature of the *interest rate gap*. Historically, although the terminology may vary somewhat, the essential variables are the *normal* loan rate and the *natural rate* of interest:

1. **The Normal Loan Rate:** It is easy to confuse "loan rate" with "bank loan rate" but they are entirely different in the classical view. Wicksell defined the "normal" loan rate as: "That loan rate that is a direct expression of the real rate, we call the normal rate." (Wicksell: 192 as cited by Salerno 2016) This normal loan rate also appears to be identical to what Ricardo (1826) called the *market rate of interest* –the loan rate dependent upon the rate of profits (see *natural interest* just below).   In current language, many might refer to these normal/market rates of interest as *free-market* loan rates in which interest rates are determined without interference or distortions between borrowers and lenders; these rates are expected to reflect rates of return of firms in conformity with the classical view. For the purposes of this study, the suggested term is *undistorted rates of interest* which would also

imply that the rates are determined without external, coercive influence (including via the creation of fiat money)

*Note: When referring to interest rates, there is often an apparent arbitrary mixing of singular and plural; in a free loan market, because many interest rates are believed to exist simultaneously, rather than a single interest rate determined by a central institution, plural is considered more appropriate. However as shall be discussed in loan rate determination absent distortions, the final loan rate negotiated between a borrower and lender could reasonably considered to be singular.

2. **The Natural Rate of Interest (NRI)** or *real interest rate*. The normal loan rate (above) derives from natural interest which has be described as the *rate of profits*, the *(expected) rate of return on investment, expected profitability of capital investment* of firms, or the *expected yield*. Ropke (1936) called it a "...fictitious figure, reflecting roughly the average rate of profits anticipated from capital investment...." (1936:114-115). (Also Re: Bohm-Bawerk 1901 and Fetter 1914).

Keynes (1936), instead of using the terms natural/real rate of interest, coined the term *marginal efficiency of capital* (MEC) for "...the expected rate of return on investment — which is nothing other than Wicksell's natural rate." (Salerno 2016)

Distinction: Bank Loan Rate and Normal Loan Rate. As distinct from the normal loan or market loan rate detailed above, the *bank loan rate* is defined simply as: "...the rate at which they (banks) are willing to lend (money)." (Ricardo: 364). Ricardo emphasizes the distinction between the *normal loan rate* (though he called it the *market rate* or *interest for money*) and *bank loan rate*: The interest for money is "...not regulated by the rate at which the Bank will lend, whether it be 5, 4, or 3 percent., but by *the rate of profits* which can be made by the employment of capital, and which is totally independent of the quantity, or the value of money." (Ricardo: 363). (emphasis added)

Convergence: Natural Closing of the Interest Rate Gap. At some point an *equilibrium* (interest rate) is expected to be reached in which there is a convergence between normal loan rates and rates of return as part of the process of adjustment between supply and demand: "The rate of interest at which the demand for loan capital and the supply of savings exactly agree ... more or less corresponds to the *expected yield* on the newly created capital." (Wicksell 1898:192 as cited by Salerno 2016). (emphasis added)

Consequences of Interest Rate Gaps

When bank lending rates are too low relative to natural interest rates, credit inflation and boom and bust cycles are theorized to result. Ricardo (1826) was clear on the consequences of bank lending at rates below market rates: "If they (banks) charge less than the market rate of interest, there is no amount of money which they might not lend...The reason, then, why for the last twenty years, the Bank is said to have given so much aid to commerce, by assisting the merchants with money, is because they have, during that whole period, lent money below the market rate of interest...." (Ricardo 1826: 364)

Notably, Wicksell's work on the interest rate gap forms a foundation of the Austrian theory of the business cycle (Mises 1912, Huerta de Soto 2012; Re: *Austrian Business Cycle Theory*)) which helps explain the phenomenon of *booms and busts* that continue to this day; the systemic problem of *financialization* and reliance on debt-based growth has been described as well (Stockman 2013) which may underlie overall signs of economic and social decline as well (Ferguson 2014).

In the 1930's, considerable debate ensued among economists (Lindahl 1939, Myrdal 1939, Hayek 1931) regarding inflation impacts and the interest rate gap. Keynes (1936) also weighed in on the matter by replacing the natural rate by the "neutral" or "optimum" rate of interest and linking them to the state of full employment (in modern terms, *potential GDP*).

Discounting and Asset Price Inflation. It is also important to note that Keynes' marginal efficiency of capital (MEC) as well as the *rate of return over cost* (Fisher 1907, 1930) relate to the critical concept of *discounting*, the *discount rate* being the rate of return that brings a stream of future cash flows to the present: The *present value* (PV) can be expressed as follows:

$$PV = NCF_1/(1+r) + NCF_2/(1+r^2)+...+NCF_n/(1+r^n)$$

...where NCF is the future *net cash flow*, and r is the rate of return/discount rate. For a stream of income, this discount rate/rate of return can also be referred to as the *internal rate of return* (IRR) and which is used to compute the "yield" or more formally the *yield to maturity* on a bond (YTM). The IRR was studied in Kennedy (2016) and is updated and compared to the *rate of return on cost* (RRC) in Appendix 2). Also refer to Damodaran 2012, Fabozzi 2011, Rosenbaum and Pearl 2013.

As can be seen from the formula above, the problem with the arbitrary control of interest rates is that they are tied to *present value*, whether or not the value is justified. In the classical view, policy interest rates that are set lower than natural rates of return can lead to rising present values of assets, asset price inflation and booms that exacerbate unjust wealth inequality, followed by collapses in asset prices, bankruptcies, and banking crises. (Re: Sigurjónsson 2015).

While lower policy rates *appear* to stimulate growth by making additional borrowing more "affordable," because of the linkage between interest/discount rate and present values as shown above, additional borrowings tend to simply purchase *appreciated* assets. Apart from very early borrowers, most borrowers may be simply buying overpriced assets that require *more* (low-cost) debt to purchase.

Deteriorating Returns and Stagnation. Although not obvious, over the long-term, sustained low policy rates also send a signal that may encourages declining returns of firms and economic stagnation. (Andrews, et al. 2017; Borio and Disyatat 2014; Chi 2017; Ferguson 2014; Hale 2015; McCormick 2016; Shedlock 2017; Also re: corporate *zombification*).
Refer to the chart below of yields on 90-day (3-month) U.S. Treasury Bills (Re: *riskfree rate*) from 1982-2017 for a visualization of the historical trend of policy interest rates.

9

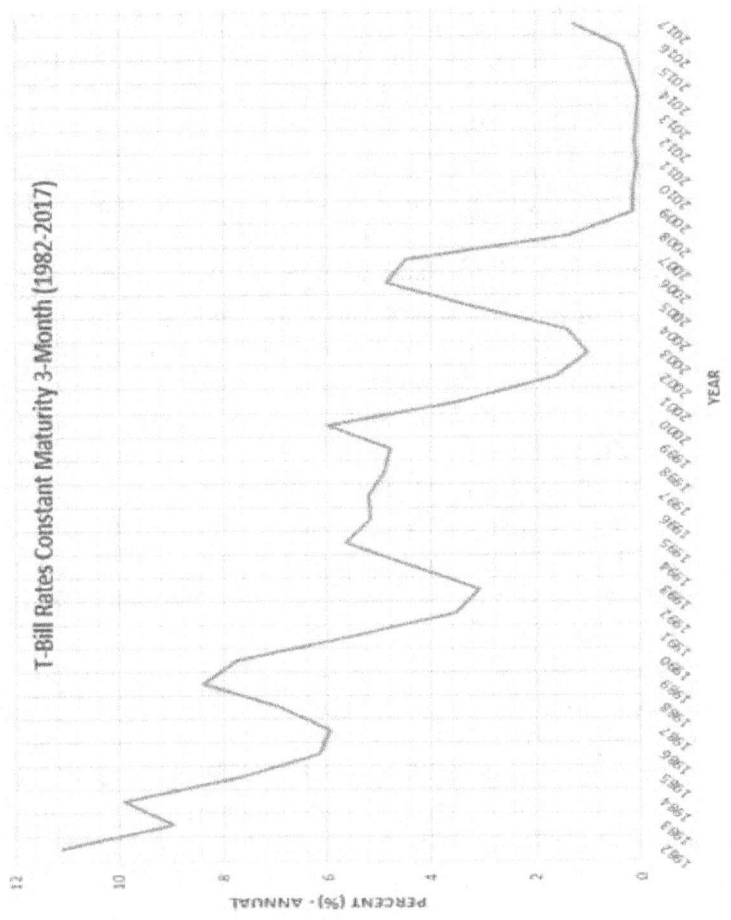

Source of Data: Federal Reserve *Selected Interest Rates - H.15* Historical Data (Annual); Market Yield on U.S. Treasury securities at 3-month constant maturity, quoted on investment basis.

The Modern Interest Rate Gap and Neutrality

Wicksell's references to *neutrality* may have served as a springboard and guideline for monetary policymaking. Some examples from Wicksell are provided here:

"So long as prices remain unaltered the [central] banks' rate of interest is to remain unaltered. If prices rise, the rate of interest is to be raised; and if prices fall, the rate of interest is to be lowered…." (1898:189 as cited in Manrique and Marqués 2004).

"As the *representative monetary rate of interest* converges on the natural rate, it becomes neutral with respect to the level and structure of real economic activity." (Wicksell 1898 as cited in Trautwein 2008). (Italics added for emphasis)

By the turn of the 21st century, the term *natural* interest rate was dominant among monetary policymakers (Holston, Laubach and Williams 2016; Laubach and Williams 2003, 2015; Lundvall and Westermark 2011). Modern estimates of the natural interest (e.g. the Laubach-Williams framework) make use of various macroeconometric modeling approaches.

As for current estimates of the natural rate, Brainard (2015) states: "Laubach and Williams…estimate that the natural rate, a concept closely related to the neutral rate, likely will remain near zero for the foreseeable future."

The Neutral Interest Rate and Gap. The closely related term *neutral interest rate* draws from Keynes and is an important guide for monetary policy, defined as follows: "The nominal neutral interest rate is the level of the federal funds rate that is consistent with output growing close to its potential rate with full employment and stable inflation." …. "The appropriate pace and target for normalizing monetary policy depend centrally on understanding the neutral rate of interest." (Brainard 2015).

With respect to a modern definition of the interest rate gap, it is the discrepancy between the policy rate and the estimated neutral rate: "The appropriate benchmark for assessing the stance of monetary policy is the gap between the policy rate and the nominal neutral rate of interest: When the federal funds rate is below the nominal neutral rate, monetary policy is accommodative, and, when it is above the neutral rate, policy is contractionary. For this reason, many monetary policy rules, such as the well-known Taylor rule, incorporate an estimate of the neutral real interest rate as a critical parameter along with the target rate of inflation." (Brainard 2015)

11

With regards to current estimates, Clarida (2017) states "…the equilibrium (neither accommodative nor restrictive) neutral real policy rate consistent with full employment and the Fed's 2% PCE inflation target, is at present around 0%."

Reflections

Distortive Causes and Impacts. Regarding the classical view, the existence of interest rate gaps may not always produce immediate and observable undesirable effects, or even effects of similar magnitudes each time they occur, but there is a believed to be strong *likelihood* of system-wide economic distortions occurring over extended periods of time. Based on the classical analysis, the banking system and modern banks are *external* interventions into markets for loanable funds, decoupled from interest rate determination through natural rates/natural rates of return. As a potential source of interest rate gaps, modern banking systems, including central banks and *fractional reserve banking*, could be viewed as a source of systemic distortion within economies.

Logical Circularity. Regarding the modern version, Spitznagel (2017) notes a fundamental *circularity problem* with neutral interest rates. " Moreover, they are using observable data as model inputs that are the result of interventions that are already in effect."

Interest Rates as Infinite. The problem with a single *policy interest rate* was highlighted in Kennedy (2015) in the context of credit-based interest rates. It was argued that interest rates are in fact innumerable, reflecting the dynamics of individual financial entities (e.g. businesses). A single policy interest rate means that there is a likelihood of interest rate gaps existing for some firms and not for others. The only way to overcome this is for individual rates to emerge. The extension of a microeconomic approach to interest rates (firm-specific natural interest) is discussed further below.

The next section (Part II) details a microeconomic approach to interest rates, introduced in Kennedy (2015) with credit-based interest rates (CBI).

Part II. A Microeconomic Approach to Interest Rate Determination

The following table of interest rate determination theories summarizes the historical and modern views seen in Part I, then revisits the microeconomic approach of *credit-based interest rates* (CBI) presented in Kennedy (2015).

CBIs have a second more complex dimension termed "credit-based natural interest rates" (CNRI) to be introduced and elaborated upon at length later in this section.

The 4th approach noted in the table, referred to as Credit and Market-Based, is theoretical and posits an undistorted financial environment which may not be easily (or ever) fully achieved but which serves as a general guide for understanding financial distortions and their absence, to be further discussed in Part II (B).

Throughout this Part II, refer to the **Interest Rate Determination Theories Table** below (also abbreviated as Interest Rate Theory Table):

Interest Rate Determination: Summary

Section	APPROACHES	Interest Rate Type	Derivation/direct expression of	Based on Measure(s):
Part I	**#1. Classical** *E.g. Cantillon (1755); Smith (1776); Ricardo (1826); Wicksell (1898);* *Mises (1912); Fetter (1914).*	Normal Loan Rate, Market Rate	Real or Natural Rate of Interest	Expected rate of return on investment, yield, rate of profits.
	#2. Modern: Macroeconomic Modeling and Policymaking Bank Loan Rates (banking system) *E.g. Fisher (1907, 1931); Keynes (1936); Von Neumann (1945);* *CGE, DSGE models (various, e.g. Romer 2012; Dixon-Jorgenson 2013)*		Policy Interest Rate	Macroeconomic/Industry factors *as determined by policymakers and modelers*
Part II (A)	**#3. Microeconomic: Credit-Based, Firm-Specific**			
	#3a. *Kennedy (2015)*	Credit-Based (Existing Debt) (CBI)	Debt service capacity (Schedule: Interest and Principal)	Source of Repayment (SOR)= NNCF-D (firm-specific), Principal, Amortization, DSC Ratio
	#3b. *Kennedy (this document)*	Credit-Based, Natural Interest (CNRI) (Qualifying Loan Amount and interest rate)	**Two elements combined to produce the CNRI:** 1. Debt service capacity (Schedule: Interest and Principal) 2. Natural Rates of Return	Rate of Return on Cost (RRC); dynamic stochastic
Part II (B)	**#4. Undistorted Credit and Other Markets, Firm-specific**		Natural Rates of Return (NRR) (see 3b. CNRI above)	As negotiated by market* participants *(Assumption: undistorted markets)*

Undistorted: totality of true cost of financing and opportunity costs reflected

(A) Credit-Based Interest Rates, Firm Specific (Static Cases)

This section corresponds to Approach #3 in the Interest Rate Theory table above.

Credit-based interest rates are comprised of two forms:

1. **Existing Debt Loads.** The interest rate computed when firms have existing debt loads to be refinanced;

2. **Qualifying Loan Amount**. How much debt (linked to the corresponding interest rate) a firm can theoretically qualify for.

(A.1) Credit-Based Interest Rates (CBI): Existing Debt Loads

This section corresponds to Approach #3a in the Interest Rate Theory table above.

In Kennedy (2015) *credit-based interest* rates (CBIs) were introduced to compute interest rates for non-financial firms with an *existing* debt load subject to a hypothetical refinance. To compute the CBI, the principal balance is *already known*. CBIs are thought to be influenced or "led" by policy rates, and may not correspond properly to the debt service capacity of firms as policy potentially incentivizes them to borrow beyond their means.

Some key takeaways regarding the concept of CBIs from that study are summarized here:

1. **Firm-Specific.** Each financial entity (businesses) is treated as an individual unit upon which the CBI is computed. Because there are countless entities, #2 below follows:

2. **Innumerable interest rates**. There is no single credit-based interest rate; the computed CBIs are as diverse as the financial entities that borrow. Therefore, interest rates should more correctly be referred to in the plural, not singular, form.

3. **Policy rate Impact and CBI Gap.** Firms in some sectors were unable to service a hypothetical refinance of their existing debt loads, raising the question as to what induced them to take on more debt than they could service. This may confirm the relevance of above-mentioned interest rate "gap", suggesting that the over-indebtedness of firms may be in part "led" by policy. For example, as policy interest rates decline over time, some firms may be more

15

likely to take on additional debt to finance their activities. It is reasonable to assume that even firms experiencing some financial stress might borrow at low rates as a substitute for income in hopes of better financial performance later.

In turn, the increased debt loads influenced by policy rates may have the secondary effect of reducing credit-based interest rates over the long term. Recall that the CBIs are computed based on the amount of debt to be refinanced, the firm's *source of repayment* (SOR)* to sufficiently cover debt service (principal + interest) at a given debt service coverage (DSC) ratio, and the amortization of the loan. The SOR is equity income less dividends; this is reviewed further below in this section, with background details in Appendix 2 drawing originally from Kennedy (2015).

As a firm's debt load increases, it is not a foregone conclusion that the source of repayment for debt can automatically match the additional amount of debt service required—at best there could be a lag before the source of repayment catches up. Therefore, as policy interest rates have approached the zero lower bound, CBIs also might also be expected to decline for the firms that have taken on increasing debt loads in response to the lower policy rates.

Sample Computation of the CBI: Static Case

The following example is based on a *static* figure for the primary source of repayment (SOR) which is intended to simplify the discussion (Part IV is an attempt to address this with a dynamic stochastic approach).

Refer to the CBI Table and CBI Chart that accompany the explanations here.

10-Year Term Loan, Matching Amortization, DSC=1.5x

The CBI Table below shows the steps towards computing the credit-based interest rate (CBI) as originally introduced in Kennedy (2015). The example here is for a 10-year term loan which fully amortizes at the end of the term (10/10), and for a debt service coverage (DSC) ratio of 1.5:1 (also written as 1.5x). The DSC ratio is defined as SOR/DS where SOR is the primary source of repayment and DS is the debt service, defined as the payment comprised of principal + interest. Further details are provided after the table. Recall that for firms in an economy there is no *single* credit-based interest rate as every firm is expected to behave differently: "All economic entities are expected to have their own interest rate and no single "universal" interest rate can be said to exist because business cash flows vary from firm to firm and over time." (Kennedy 2015: 39)

CBI (Existing Debt Load) Computation Review Table

#	CREDIT-BASED INTEREST RATE (CBI) COMPUTATION REVIEW	10-yr Term Loan Fully-Amortizing; DSC=1.5x
1	Source of Repayment (SOR)-Annual	25
	SOR=Equity Income less Dividends	
2	Principal (P)	
2a	Initial Principal Balance	$100.00
2b	Term/Maturity (in years)	10
2c	Principal Balance at end of term	$0.0
2d	Amortization (No# of Payments)*	120
	Schedule of 120 monthly payments to be made over	
	the 10-year term (=10 years x 12 months/yr)	
3	P/SOR	4
4	Interest (Annual Rate, Amount)	
4a	Credit-based Interest Rate (Computed)	0.110
4b	Interest *Amount* Paid over Loan Term	($65.54)
5	Debt Service Amount (P+ i) -Annual	($16.55)
5a	Debt Service Amount - Monthly	($1.38)
6	Debt Service Coverage Ratio (Computed)	1.51

1. Source of Repayment (SOR)

The source of repayment (SOR) is the *primary* source of repayment for the loan, which is *equity income* less dividends.

To review, *equity income* is defined as the firm's *net net cash flow* (NNCF) (Kennedy 2016: 82-88). NNCF an extension of NCF (Kennedy 2014:3-6; Kennedy 2015: 78-80) that deducts *acquisitions, intangibles, and other key investments* in addition to capital expenditures (Capex).

The ability of a firm to service a debt can be called *debt service capacity* (DSC), typically based on *annual* figures. The DSC is based on *NNCF less dividends* as the primary source of repayment, and the amount of debt to be serviced (=principal plus interest).

The SOR figure of 25 currency units in the table is arbitrary and is an annual figure of *equity income* less dividends which is assumed to be the amount available to pay back the loan. For simplicity, the SOR figure is treated as static and stochastic processes are not assumed: It is recognized that this is not realistic. Therefore, an attempt at addressing randomness in the variable(s) is found in the main text in the discussion on firm-specific natural interest rates.

The term *cash flow* or *net cash flow* might loosely be used; however, in relationship to debt service capacity *equity income less dividends* (Re: Source of repayment SOR*)* is more accurate. (Also recall that for *capacity to pay dividends*, equity income is viewed as central; Re: Kennedy 2014).

2. Principal (P)

This section (2a-2d) relates to the loan: The initial principal balance, the term/maturity in years, the principal balance at the end of the term (which if fully amortizing loan should be zero), and the number of payments.

The figure of 100 currency units is also arbitrary.

3. Principal /Source of Repayment Multiple (P/SOR)

The P/SOR is most commonly a single digit from say 2 to 6, but for some firms with little equity income) and high debt, could go into the double digits, or can be undefined or negative if the SOR is zero or negative, respectively. The P/SOR is simply computed as Principal/SOR; the figure of "4" for the P/SOR is (100/25) =4. In words, a P/SOR multiple of 4 means that the principal balance of the loan is four times greater than the annual primary source of repayment (SOR) amount (from Kennedy (2015; further modified in Kennedy 2016). The primary SOR is defined as NNCF *less dividends/distributions* (See Appendix 2 for a brief overview).

Recall from Kennedy (2015) that the *credit-based interest rate* (CBI, *y-axis* below) was computed with the formula for the payment of an ordinary annuity, $PMT=r(P_0)/1-(1+r)^{-n}$ based on selected P/SOR multiples (which are on the *x-axis*: 1 to 5). The CBI, labelled "interest rate," is on the *y*-axis and is computed using the following criteria: The P/SOR multiple for a given (existing) loan amount to be refinanced and the lender's required debt service coverage ratio (DSC ratio) of 1.5:1 for a 10-year fully amortizing loan. The chart here has been improved for clarity (Kennedy 2015: 33).

CBI at Various P/SOR Multiples

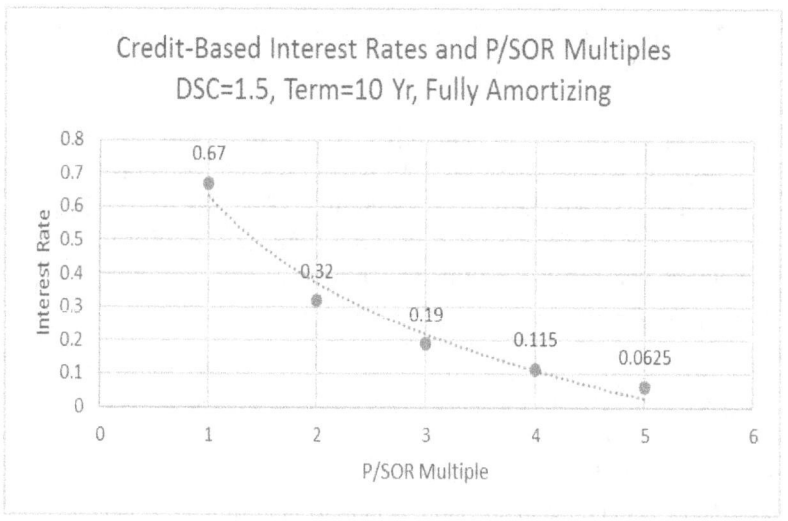

CBI in 3-Dimensional Format (P/SOR=4) The above 2-dimensional chart can be converted to a 3-dimensional one as shown below by isolating a single *principal/source of repayment* (P/SOR) multiple to show the relationship between the computed credit-based interest rate (CBI) on the z-axis, the loan term/amortization (assumed to be matching, and labelled only "term") in years on the x-axis, and the debt service coverage ratio (DSC ratio) on the y-axis. The chart below is for a Principal/SOR multiple of 4 (note that if printed in black in white some detail may be lost):

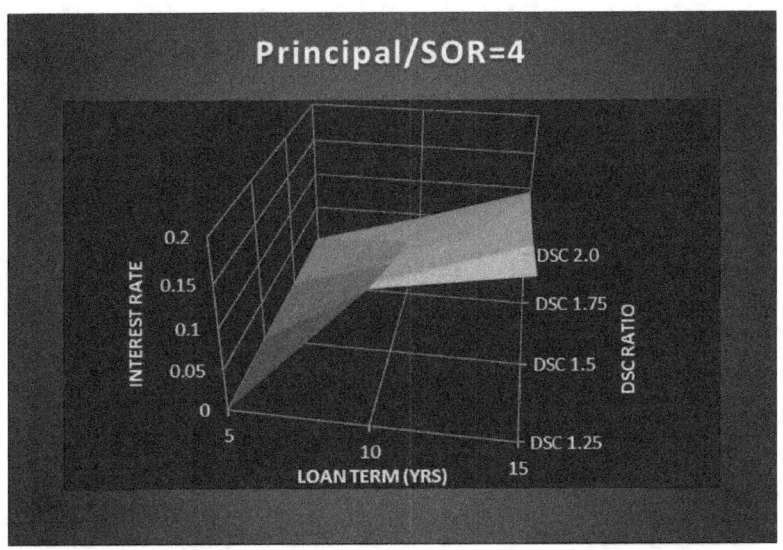

4. Interest (CBI Annual Rate, Amount): Computed
CBI with Fitted Exponential Formula

In Kennedy 2015 (42-43), the CBI for any *intermediate* P/SOR multiples (i.e. those values between 1, 2, 3, 4, and 5) were computed by *linear interpolation*. This approach was acknowledged as rudimentary, and is modified below by fitting the data to an exponential curve, explained next. By using the computed data points for selected P/SORs (1, 2, 3, 4, 5…) an exponential equation can be fitted of the form:

$$y=bm^x$$

…where b is a constant and the y-intercept, x is the exponent, and the *m* values are bases corresponding to a given exponent's value. The P/SOR is the input provided as the exponent.

DSC 1.5, 10/10 Case. For a DSC of 1.5 and a 10-year fully-amortizing loan (10-year term with 10-year matching amortization), the fitted formula was $y = (1.108)(0.5617)^x$ based on the actual, manually-computed data points of P/SOR multiples 1 through 6. The actual vs. predicted values for the CBI based on this fitted exponential curve are shown in the chart below:

20

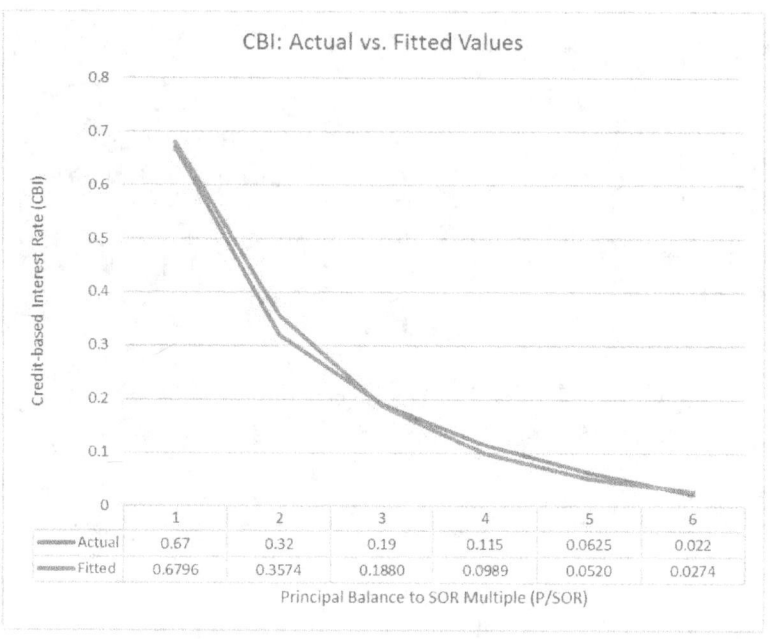

CBI: Actual vs. Fitted Values

Principal Balance to SOR Multiple (P/SOR)	1	2	3	4	5	6
Actual	0.67	0.32	0.19	0.115	0.0625	0.022
Fitted	0.6796	0.3574	0.1880	0.0989	0.0520	0.0274

The computed credit-based interest rate (CBI) based on the fitted exponential curve shown above is 11% per annum, slightly below the *actual* computed figure of 11.5% corresponding to a P/SOR of 4 (recall that this CBI is estimated from the *fitted curve*, not on the actual data).

5. Debt Service Amount (Annual)

The debt service is defined as the principal to be repaid each repayment period (e.g. monthly) plus the interest owed. The debt service amount to be paid *annually* is the monthly amount multiplied by 12 months, and is shown as $16.55.

This annual debt service is computed with the ordinary annuity formula as noted above, $PMT = r(P_0)/1-(1+r)^{-n}$, using the following figures: The computed CBI from #4 above of 0.11, the number of payments of 120 (120 monthly payments are made over the 10-year term), and the initial principal balance of 100 currency units in #2a. For an annual figure, the monthly figure is multiplied by 12.

21

Multiplying the annual debt service by 10 years yields a total amount to be paid (both principal to be returned plus the interest) of $165.54; that total less the initial principal balance of the loan of 100 is $65.54. The debt service breakdown is summarized in the table below:

Initial Principal Balance	100
Annual Debt Payment (monthly x 12)	($16.55)
Years of Amortization	10
Total Amount Paid (P+i)	($165.54)
Principal Portion	100
Interest Portion	($65.54)

6. Debt Service Coverage (DSC) Ratio (*computed*)

The DSC ratio is computed by dividing the annual SOR (#1) by the annual debt service amount (#5) or 25/16.55=1.51. This should correspond very closely to the required 1.5x debt service coverage ratio (*required by the lender*) upon which the fitted curve is based upon.

(A.2) Credit-Based, Natural Interest Rates (CNRI): Static Case

The *credit-based natural rate of interest* is also written as *credit-based natural interest rate* and abbreviated CNRI. This section covers #3a in the Interest Rate Theory table above.

Recall that in the CBI computation above, the loan amount is *known* because it is *existing debt* assumed to be refinanced, leaving the interest rate (i.e. the credit-based interest rate or CBI) to be computed.

The credit-based natural rate of interest (CNRI) computation focuses on taking on *additional debt* to arrive at a total *qualifying amount* of debt at a given interest rate. There are two essential and intertwined elements to arriving at the CNRI: These are referred to as "Element 1" and "Element 2" to be detailed below.

1. *Debt Service capacity* (DSC). The lender determines what debt service coverage (DSC) is desired and how much more debt the

borrower can take on at a given interest rate (this can include loan consolidation and rolling *existing* debt into a larger loan amount); 2. *Natural Rates of Return* (NRR). The NRR is a starting point from which both borrower and lender might be expected to negotiate and find an interest rate "match" that they can agree upon; this is a *market-negotiated* rate, and these rates are firm-specific. CNRIs and the NRRs that they are assumed to be based upon in some way are as numerous as the number of financial entities in existence (i.e. potentially infinite).

These two essential elements are further detailed below.

Element 1. Debt Service Capacity. A fundamental basis for creditworthiness and qualifying for a loan is overall *debt service capacity*, based on the lender requirement for *debt service coverage*. The CNRI attempts to answer the question of "how much can I (the firm) borrow *and* at what rate?" Initially we compute hypothetical loan amounts and interest rates that conform to the required debt service coverage (DSC) ratio of the lender, to be done just below in the example on loan qualification.

However, the *final* loan amount or interest rate will not be known until agreed upon until the terms are negotiated in a market for loanable funds. This is addressed in Element 2 further below.

CNRI Loan Qualification Example (Static Case)

Review of Factors and Constraints in Credit Extension. The scenario below illustrates the mechanics of financing/extending credit to answer the question of how much the borrower can qualify for. The inputs remain the same as in the CBI example above:

1. The **term** and **amortization** of the loan are assumed to be both 10 years and 10 years, respectively (i.e. "matching term and amortization" and written as 10/10).

2. The lender's desired/required **debt service coverage (DSC) ratio** is assumed to be 1.5x. This ratio is arbitrarily chosen as an approximation of an "intermediate" level of debt service capacity.

Recall that the DSC ratio is defined as SOR/DS where the numerator SOR is the primary source of repayment for the loan: *NNCF* less *dividends* (NNCF being termed "equity income"). The denominator DS refers to *debt service*, defined as the sum of *principal and interest* (Kennedy 2015: 27-28).

Refer to the CNRI Schedule and CNRI Table in the discussion below.

The CNRI Schedule

The CNRI Schedule is a schedule of the interest rate against the principal balance of the loan (i.e. the initial loan amount) expressed as a *proportion* of the maximum principal balance (Pmax) at which the interest rate is zero.

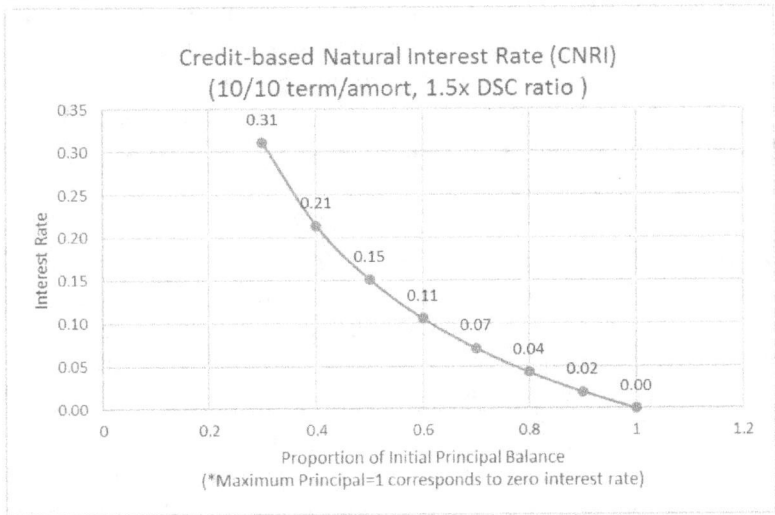

Since both the interest rate and the loan balance are unknown, the CNRI refers to a *schedule* – various *potential* interest rates at various *potential* quantities of credit to be lent/borrowed within the constraints of credit guidelines (i.e. debt service capacity for a given amortization term). Thus, rather than referring to the CNRI as single "rate" in the singular form, multiple potential "rates" expressed in the *plural* form might be more accurate: CNRIs.

Discrete vs. Continuous. The chart shows a continuous curve for ease of visibility. However, it should be emphasized that while a curve may be convenient for mathematical modeling, in real-world decision-making there may be no continuous curve at all— rather, the schedule should more correctly show a set of *discrete points*.

Interest Rate and Economization in Financing. As *less* is borrowed (*economizing* on borrowings), the interest rate that the firm can afford to pay (in terms of debt service capacity =1.5x) rises. The greater the amount of borrowings the lower the interest rate (to a maximum principal balance at which the interest rate becomes zero). **Incentives.** There is a built-in incentive for lenders to economize on loanable funds/resources since the interest rate (rate of return for the lender) declines as more loanable funds are lent out. As the borrowing amount increases, the interest rate declines, which reflects the *weakening* borrowing capacity of the borrower to service the (greater) debt load. This fundamental relationship acts as a critical disincentive to lend excessively.

The CNRI Table and Computation Review

Total Qualifying Amount. The lender requires a minimum DSC ratio of 1.5x. Given the firm's SOR (Line 1) of 25, the loan amortization of 120 monthly payments at 2.5% interest per annum, then the firm can qualify for 150 as the initial amount of the loan (Line 2a); currency units are represented by $ signs).

Debt Consolidation. If the firm already carries 100 of debt on its books to be consolidated into the new larger loan of 150, then the *additional* amount it can borrow is 50 (150 qualifying at 2.5% annual interest-100 existing to be consolidated and refinanced=50).

The CNRI Table followed by the line-item detail is shown next with the aim of maintaining the logical order of steps.

#	CNRI TABLE / COMPUTATION REVIEW TERMS	10-yr Term Loan Fully-Amortizing, DSC=1.5
1	Source of Repayment (SOR)-Annual	25
2	Principal (P)	
2a	Qualifying Amount (per CNRI, schedule: See 4a)	$150.00
2b	Term/Maturity (in years)	10
2c	Principal Balance at end of term	$0.0
2d	Amortization (No# of Payments)*	120
2e	PMax*-Principal Balance at Zero Interest	$166.67
	*given the desired DSC coverage ratio (#6a)	
3	P/SOR	6.00
3a	Proportion of PMax	0.9
4	Interest (Annual Rate, Amount)	
4a	Interest Rate (CNRI, Computed; CNRI Schedule)	0.025
4b	Interest *Amount* Paid over Loan Term	($6.59)
5	Debt Service Amount (P+ i) -Annual	($16.98)
5a	Debt Service Amount - Monthly	($16.98)
5b	DSMax -Maximum Debt Service Amount (Annua	$16.67
6	Debt Service Coverage (DSC) Ratio-Computed	1.47
6a	Debt Service Coverage (DSC) Ratio-Desired	1.5

#6a Debt Service Coverage (DSC)-Desired by Lender

This is a lender requirement, set at a DSC ratio of 1.5x.
Note that #6, the DSC ratio-computed figure is computed at the very end after the desired amount of the loan and interest rate have been decided upon.

#5b DSMax – Maximum debt service amount (annual)

Given the DSC Ratio specified in #6a, the maximum debt service amount that would be acceptable to the lender based on the SOR of the firm of 25 (in line item #1) is $16.67 per year.

#2e PMax – Principal balance at zero interest rate

Given the desired DSC coverage ratio (#6a) which gives a DSMax (#5b) of $16.67, the maximum principal balance assuming a zero interest rate would be $166.67 for the 10-year fully-amortizing term of the loan.

#3a Proportion of PMax

The maximum principal balance in #2e above is sized to the number "1" (again, corresponding to a zero interest rate) and adjusted as desired. In an undistorted environment, lenders would be expected to seek an interest rate greater than zero, and their opportunity cost will figure into the decision-making process to be noted further below.

#4a Interest rate (CNRI, Computed; Refer to Schedule)

Once the Proportion of PMax (#3a) has been decided, then the initial principal balance (#2a) and the corresponding interest rate (#4a) are now known. In this example, the proportion decided upon was 0.90 giving an initial principal balance of 150 and an interest rate of 0.025 (or 2.5%) per annum. The interest rate (CNRI) of 0.025 was computed by fitting an exponential curve as explained next.

Fitted Exponential Curve: DSC 1.5x, 10/10 Case. An exponential curve was fitted of the form:

$$y=bm^x$$

...where b is a constant and the y-intercept, x is the exponent, and the m values are bases corresponding to a given exponent's value. Line item **#3a Proportion of PMax** from the CNRI table is the input provided as the exponent.

For a DSC Ratio of 1.5x and a 10-year fully-amortizing loan (10-year term with 10-year matching amortization or "10/10"), the fitted formula was $y=1.295*(0.01254)^x$ based on the actual data points for **PMax** of 1, 0.9, 0.8....0.3 and their corresponding actual interest rates. The data used to fit the exponential curve were manual computations in a spreadsheet and were *not estimates*.

Actual vs. Predicted Values. The actual vs. predicted values for the CNRI based on this fitted exponential curve are shown in the chart below, for reference. A substantial discrepancy between fitted and actual values is acknowledged.

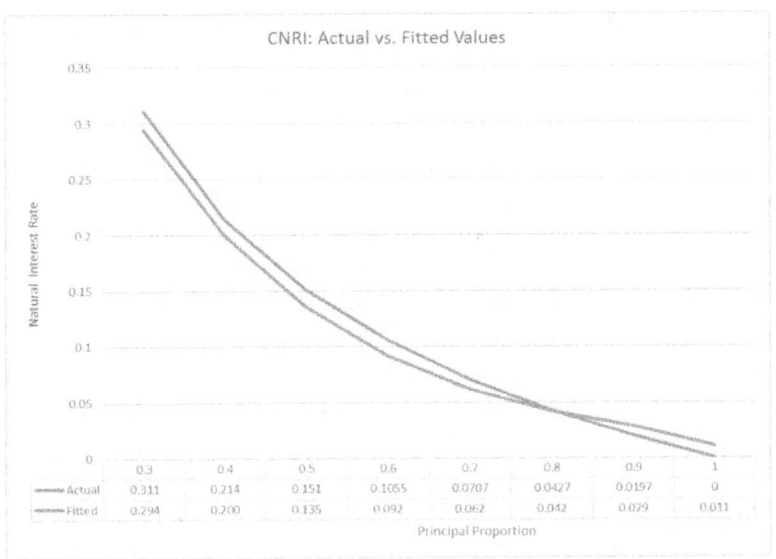

	0.3	0.4	0.5	0.6	0.7	0.8	0.9	1
Actual	0.311	0.214	0.151	0.1055	0.0707	0.0427	0.0197	0
Fitted	0.294	0.200	0.135	0.092	0.062	0.042	0.029	0.011

CNRI: Actual vs. Fitted Values (y-axis: Natural Interest Rate; x-axis: Principal Proportion)

Debt Service Ratio Check

Returning to the CNRI schedule above and the corresponding line items in the table, we have the following:

Line Items #3a and #4a. The data points on the y and x axes, respectively, are the *interest rate** and *proportion of the principal balance** where the firm can *exactly* service the debt for a 10-year term with matching amortization (10/10) at a debt service coverage ratio (DSC ratio) of 1.5 times the source of repayment (SOR) of the firm.

*The interest rate and proportion of the principal balance correspond to **#4a Interest Rate (CNRI, Computed) and #3a Proportion of PMax**, respectively, in the CNRI table, above.

#2e PMax-Principal Balance at Zero Interest. An interest rate of 0 corresponds to an x-axis ordinate of 1. The figure 1 refers to the *maximum principal balance* that the firm can service, which is at a zero interest rate: At this loan amount, the firm can only repay the loan if the interest rate is zero given a 10-year term with matching amortization and a debt service ratio of 1.5x.

28

Adjusting Quantity of Credit. As the amount of debt declines, the firm is more able to "afford" (i.e. service) the lower debt and therefore can in theory pay a *higher* rate of interest. This will be covered in **Element 2** of the CNRI calculus below; the actual quantity of credit to be extended is ultimately *unknown* until determined through negotiation in the loanable funds market. The borrower may not be willing to accept the loan amount offered and/or the interest rate for the amount of credit extended. The lender also may not be willing to commit too much loanable funds at too low an interest rate (rate of return).

#6. Creditworthiness Check: DSC Ratio. Line Item **#6**, titled the **Debt Service Coverage (DSC) Ratio-Computed** is computed at the very end after the amount of the loan and interest rate have been decided upon: The estimated DSC ratio is 1.47 which approximates the lender's required 1.5x. If all other lender criteria for borrower creditworthiness are met, this loan appears to qualify in this simple example at 2.5% interest.

Element 2. Natural Rates of Return

In addition to the creditworthiness element, a second complex element forms the basis for arriving at CNRIs: *Natural rates of return* (NRR) or *natural returns*, abbreviated. These natural rates of return are the result of at least the following key constraining factors referred also to as "constraints" to be detailed further below: 1. **Rate of Return**. The borrowing entity's *own innate rate of return*, measured here by the *firm-specific rate of return on cost* (RRC) which is *also* its *firm-specific* natural rate of return (NRR). This rate of return constitutes a theoretical upper borrowing rate limit; 2. **Market Environment**. *Opportunity cost* to the lender and the overall availability of funds in the loanable funds market. This opportunity cost constitutes a theoretical floor rate for the lender. Some part, or all the funds could be lent elsewhere at better rates of return; this leads to *credit rationing* where the supply of loanable funds to a given borrower might be adjusted based on a minimum rate of return (CNRI) desired. Refer to the example above in which the quantity of credit was adjusted; 3. **Negotiations/Wrap-Up** between borrower and lender. The final arrangement terms will not be known until negotiated by the

29

parties. (It is acknowledged that this process may eventually be *automated* to a point such that there may be little need for any drawn-out negotiations between the parties; the amounts and at which terms and conditions under which each party is willing to borrow/lend would be pre-specified and executed by programs).

CNRI Determination: Constraints

Constraining factors of Element 2 involved in ultimately arriving at the CNRI is detailed below in 3 sections.

1. Upper Limit (Borrower): Natural Rate of Return (NRR). The borrower must compare how much debt service (principal + interest as a cash outflow) will be required relative to the potential *additional income* to be earned by borrowing (cash inflow). Additional cash *inflow* is compared to the additional cash *outflow* such that the rate of return can be achieved by borrowing aligns to some degree the *firm's own rate of return* as an entity. As developed and detailed previously (Kennedy 2016), the firm-specific measure adopted for the rate of return for firms is the *rate of return on cost* (RRC); an overview of the RRC is provided in Appendix 2 on fundamentals. RRC is also the firm's own natural rate of return (NRR) (i.e. *firm specific* natural rate of return) best evaluated over *extended time periods*, particularly when considering term lending (term loans).

Additional Points for Clarification.

Return=Cost. Although somewhat confusing, the rate of *return* can simultaneously be viewed as a *cost* (the RRC). This however can be understood from the standpoint of *opportunity cost*. For example, if a firm's RRC is 10%, this also represents a cost in the sense of what is "lost" (given up) if the firm ceases activity; the higher the return, the more that the firm stands to lose (higher opportunity cost).

From a *financing* standpoint, the borrower is expected to prefer financing costs that are *lower* than its own (natural) rate of return, otherwise it is more profitable to finance itself internally (which is its own internal cost of financing). Note that from a cash flow standpoint, when repaying the loan, the borrower must pay not only interest, but must pay back the *principal* (return of principal to the lender). With self-financing, there is no principal to be repaid. Therefore, the cash cost to the borrower of financing activity should also be considered.

IRR vs. RRC. It can be argued that the *internal rate of return* of the firm (IRR) also can be used as a measure of natural returns. This was addressed in Kennedy (2016), and the RRC is determined to be a reasonable proxy for IRR as reviewed in Appendix 2.

A theoretical "upper limit" (or ceiling) for interest rates from a business borrower's perspective is therefore assumed to be the rate of return on cost (RRC).

*a notable exception might be a company in distress that that wants the borrowings to fill a cash flow gap, and achieving higher returns are less important than simply keeping the company afloat.

Real vs. Nominal Interest Rates. As a reminder, in the modern view of real interest (Re: Fisher 1931) the nominal rate of interest is deducted by the rate of inflation. In the former classical view (Re: Wicksell, et al.) the natural interest rate is also the *real interest rate*. In this analysis, the firm-specific measure of the rate of return is the RRC (rate of return on cost), which is viewed as a *real* rate of return because the returns are directly linked and synchronized to *the costs* associated with the returns. Therefore, the RRC measure, as an upper limit to the CNRI, is viewed as linking real rates of return to natural interest rates on a firm-specific basis.

Assigning a Value to RRC

Since the values of the RRC (=NRR) change from year to year, arriving at an appropriate value for a theoretical upper limit presents a challenge. This is addressed in the chart and accompanying discussion below.

Theoretical Upper Limit: Relative Frequency of RRC. Up to this point, the discussion has been limited to static examples. Determining the appropriate value for the NNR (=RRC) is a challenge because the value changes from year to year. The following chart is for the *entire sample* of observations for a firm in the consumer goods sector from 1988 to 2016, a histogram which graphically describes a *relative frequency distribution* (rfd) of RRC, along with a fitted distribution overlay. This gives a visual idea of how the natural rate of return defined as RRC for the firm has behaved and shifted over time (1988-2016).

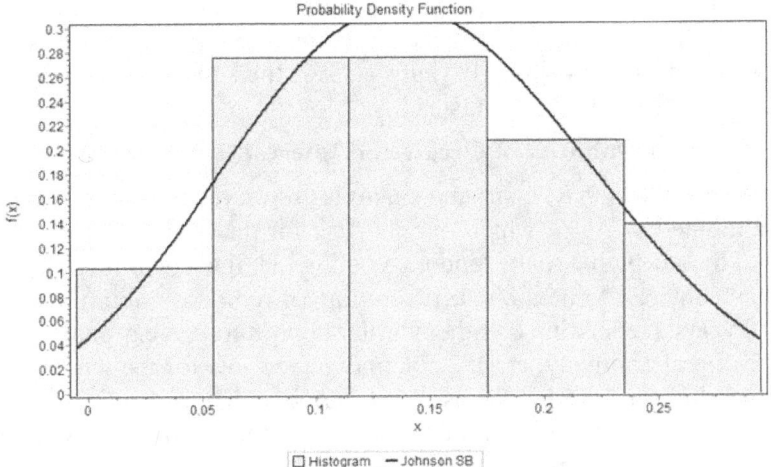

Note: The values on the *x-axis* are typically for the boundaries or mid-points of intervals or *bins* of the observations such as 0-0.0499, 0.05 to 0.099, etc. The values on the *y-axis* are the relative frequency of occurrence of the observations of RRC. In the chart above, the first bin height of about 0.10 on the y-axis means that approximately 10% of the observations fell within values between 0 and 0.05; however, figures are rough because the boundaries of the bins don't necessarily correspond to the values shown on the x-axis). Detail on distribution-fitting is found in Appendix 1.

In sum, for the *borrower*, the lower the cost of financing *relative to its own self-financed cost*, the more cash flow-*profitable* for the borrower, continuing down to a financing cost of 0%. However, given the relative frequency distribution above, it is not clear which value of RRC should be used since there have been numerous values over the years. This issue will be addressed in Part IV with a stochastic dynamic approach.

2. Lower Limit/Floor (Lender): Opportunity Cost (of Capital). Lenders expect some minimum rate of return based on competing possible uses of their capital (i.e. their loanable funds). This minimum rate of return constitutes a floor defined by what is called *opportunity cost*: What can be earned by lending elsewhere. In the example above, the CNRI interest rate computed for the loan was 2.5% per annum. The lender's opportunity cost is what it "loses" by lending at 2.5% to this borrower, committing those funds for 10 years. If other competing borrowers are able and willing to borrow for 10 years at 5%, then the lender will be induced to lend to them instead.

Adjusting Quantity of Credit and Interest Rate: Example

Again, in the CNRI chart and example above, the interest rate was computed at 2.5%. which may be fine for the borrower but may not be acceptable to the lender. As oft noted, the lender might find 2.5% interest to be an insufficient rate of return to commit to for 10 years. Depending on other similar opportunities (e.g. same risk profile of company, etc.), 2.5% may be too low for the lender. In a market for loanable funds, there may be other competing firms with strong cash flow and debt service capacity able and willing to pay higher interest rates than 2.5%.

Therefore, the lender can adjust its rate of return (the CNRI) upward by *lowering* the loan amount (Re: *credit rationing* or lowering the quantity of credit or loanable funds at its disposal) and achieving a higher rate of return on the loan (=interest rate); at the same time, the borrower can "afford" to pay that *higher* interest rate.

In this example, the lender reduces the quantity of credit (to 0.7 of the maximum Pmax) from $150 to $117 (rounded) to achieve a higher interest rate of 6%. As seen in Line 6, the DSC ratio now improves to 1.61, which exceeds the lender's desired DSC ratio of 1.5x.

CNRI Table: Adjusting Quantity of Credit and Interest Rate

#	CNRI TABLE / COMPUTATION REVIEW TERMS	10-yr Term Loan Fully-Amortizing, DSC=1.5
1	Source of Repayment (SOR)-Annual	25
2	**Principal (P)**	
2a	Qualifying Amount (per CNRI, schedule: See 4a)	$116.67
2b	Term/Maturity (in years)	10
2c	Principal Balance at end of term	$0.0
2d	Amortization (No# of Payments)*	120
2e	PMax*-Principal Balance at Zero Interest	$166.67
	*given the desired DSC coverage ratio (#6a)	
3	**P/SOR**	4.67
3a	Proportion of PMax	0.7
4	**Interest (Annual Rate, Amount)**	
4a	Interest Rate (CNRI, Computed; CNRI Schedule)	0.060
4b	Interest *Amount* Paid over Loan Term	($6.59)
5	**Debt Service Amount (P+ i) -Annual**	($15.57)
5a	Debt Service Amount - Monthly	($15.57)
5b	DSMax -Maximum Debt Service Amount (Annu	$16.67
6	**Debt Service Coverage (DSC) Ratio-Computed**	1.61
6a	Debt Service Coverage (DSC) Ratio-Desired	1.5

At a 6% interest rate, there is no assurance that the borrower will agree. Therefore, the next step involves negotiation and other factors to be discussed next.

3. Negotiations/Wrap-Up between Lender and Borrower. The interests of borrower and lender result in a compromise to arrive at *both* a final loan amount and rate of interest. As noted above, since the loan amount is linked to the firm-specific natural interest rate, for a *given* debt service (p+i) coverage it is possible for the lender to raise its return (raise the interest rate) by rationing credit i.e. lending *less* to the borrower. The borrower can lower its interest rate by increasing its borrowing amount. The final interest rate and loan amount is expected to settle somewhere along the CNRI schedule.

To simplistically illustrate the dynamics of the above, if the estimated RRC is 7% (upper limit estimate) and the borrower's desired profit margin is at least 2%, the borrower may agree to begin negotiations somewhere below 5%. The lender too has a desired spread, so that the ultimate outcome depends on the negotiations and the market conditions.

Closing Comments

While the above examples attempt to explain some of the logic involved in determining a theoretical CNRI, it is understood that this is only a very incomplete sketch of what might occur in reality. Some salient points are made here.

Debt Service with Variability and Uncertainty. For simplicity, the above discussion has avoided the topic of variability with respect to the primary source of repayment (SOR) which was simply assumed to be a fixed at 25 currency units for all 10 years of the loan. A firm's SOR can be expected to change from year to year and is an uncertain variable. Rarely would credit decisions be made based on a single fixed data point without consideration to a lengthy historical backdrop evidencing the likelihood of the firm's debt service capacity over time.

The debt service coverage ratio (in our example DSC=1.5x) is a starting point for the lender to reach a certain comfort level that the loan will be repaid. However, because of the variability and uncertainty of the source of repayment upon which the DSC ratio is based, *the lender does not want to underestimate the debt service coverage*.: The debt service (P+i) is a *fixed amount*, but the SOR can be expected to vary from year to year over the 10-year period of this hypothetical loan.

The lender fears insufficient capacity of the firm to repay the loan. This capacity is subject to many factors that could produce loan losses for the lender if the firm encounters difficulty and/or goes bankrupt. A restructuring of the loan could tie up the lender's capital for longer, possibly at a penalizing elevated rate of interest but at the cost of prolonged exposure to later losses for the lender.

How might the creditor reduce the likelihood of default or non-repayment? As already discussed, this can in part be accomplished by either *reducing* the total amount of borrowings and/or lowering the interest rate so that the *debt service* (principal + interest*) amount is lowered and easier to cover*.

However, this still does not directly address the issue of likelihood of default or non-repayment of the loan over those 10 years. As part of the credit evaluation process, lenders often attempt to forecast the firm's future debt service capacity, based often on linear loan repayment forecasts (featuring optimistic, realistic, pessimistic scenarios), but this approach falls short because the *stochastic* nature of the variables is not given consideration.

From the borrower's perspective, if the rate of return on cost (RRC) is the theoretical upper limit for an acceptable interest rate to the borrower, it is likely that the firm would not want to *overestimate the likelihood of a high rate of return* that could result in the interest rate being too high relative to the firm's own rate of return as represented by the RRC.

Financial Distortions in Brief. It should also be noted that the loanable funds market has generally been influenced by many significant distortions including the role played by the monetary and banking system; Appendix 4 provides an overview of the systemic source of distortion based on Kennedy (2017). Part II (B) is an attempt at describing the absence of distortions, although the discussion remains theoretical.

Quantity of Credit and Modern Money and Banking. Interestingly, the dynamic of credit-based and natural interest rates (CBI and CNRI) suggests that the presence of central monetary authorities and the banking system is not required for adjustments to be made to the quantity of credit and interest rates, As seen in the examples and schedules, interest rates are linked (negatively related) to the *quantity* of credit being extended to the borrower.

Decoupling of Quantity and Rates. In the current monetary and policy interest rate environment, the *quantity* of credit appears to be decoupled from interest rates. Once established, a given policy interest rate (say 2.5%, to which banks add their spreads//profit margins) the corresponding quantity of loanable funds to be lent at that policy rate is indeterminate and potentially *unlimited*. With central planning of interest rates, it is to be expected that the banking system will continue to lend as long as the loans appear to remain profitable and basic bank credit criteria are met (Kennedy 2015:4).

A framework for undistorted markets is advanced in the next section.

(B) Undistorted Credit and Other Markets

This section considers Approach #4 of the Interest Rate Theories Table above, a *theoretical* state where market and financial distortions would be absent.

A conceptual model of *economic distortion* was explored in Kennedy (2017) which incorporates distortions in the financial and monetary realm; see Appendix 4 for an overview. In brief, the absence of distortions is defined by a fundamental bond between cost and any returns associated with bearing the cost where the true and entire cost is reflected; this includes opportunity costs. Distorted markets and systems tend to involve cost shifting such that some can receive benefits/returns without the associated cost-bearing.

Currently, the data upon which analyses are based unavoidably embody economic distortions of the current paradigm, so it should be emphasized that any conclusions drawn are subject to this underlying distorted environment; the logical circularity problem involving policy was noted at the end of Part I. For evidence of financial distortions from historical data see Part III. Features of distorted/undistorted financial environments are sketched below.

Concepts

Markets vs. Undistorted Markets. A confusing point related to the problem of data noted above concerns reference to *markets* or *free markets* without consideration of underlying distortions that may be embodied in those markets. A full analysis and distinction should be made between (a) market-based systems *with underlying distortions*, and (b) market-based systems *free of distortions* (Re: Shultz 1978; also see Appendix 2 regarding rigged markets and impacts of fiat money in the bidding process).

Income does not depend on debt (Debt-Independent Growth). To stimulate economic growth, policymakers have com debt-fueled expansion typically through the lowering of policy interest rates. This involves lending not only to businesses, but individuals (Re: household debt) and governmental entities (e.g. sovereign debt). This comes with economic disruptions and other consequences noted in Part I.

Debt-Income Confusion. Excess lending/debt causes an economy-wide confusion between what is nominal income/cash flow and what is linked to real/actual income. When debt is plentiful, incomes appear to be rising; when debt based on the distortive prior *debt-income confusion* must be repaid or cannot be repaid (principal + interest), there is an unnatural counteracting force on the economy that can lead to financial and banking crises. Fixing such a distortion does not mean simply a policy change of tightening lending standards, instituting stress testing, capital requirements for banks, or *macro-prudential* lending approaches – these are stopgap policy responses that do not address the *underlying* systemic dynamic.

Removing this distortion would mean a return to a debt pricing mechanism that is expected to reflect debt service capacity naturally and more accurately. The concept of interest rates as fundamental signals that regulate (e.g. set limits on) lending behavior, coupled with undistorted markets in loanable funds, is explored later in this section with Credit-based Natural Rates of Interest (CNRI). CNRIs are based on natural rates of return (NRR), also to be examined.

Because excessive debt is viewed as a source of inflation, this would result in a reversal of a long-term policy environment of price inflation. Even if inflation rates are low or moderate, over extended periods of time an unfair wealth transfer occurs: Substantial loss of *purchasing power* for wage-earners and those living on fixed incomes (e.g. retirees), while the monetary "dilution" caused by money creation benefits debtors who can pay back their debts with depreciated currency. The reversal would move towards a secular price deflation where *existing incomes* begin to have greater purchasing power without *nominal* income rising (i.e. meaning rising *real* incomes). Savers, who experience financial repression (reduced income from low policy interest rates) and lenders also would experience rising *real* incomes from this deflationary bias. Any such a transition would be expected to take a long period of time because of the historic financialization and debt saturation of many economies, linked to fiscal problems worldwide (Re: BIS 2015, 2017; Hollingsworth 2015; Kotlikoff 2015; Stockman 2013).

Part III. Preliminary Results of Analysis

Part III begins with Section A, an exercise taking a microeconomic approach in which the firm-specific credit-based natural rate of interest (CNRI) is estimated with historical data; recall from above two elements upon which the CNRI is based: *debt service capacity* and *natural rates of return* of an actual firm. Section B examines asset mispricing in *debt* and *equities* using various analytical tools and presents the results. Section C focuses on the distortion of low-cost financing for firms that benefit from taxpayer funds without ownership recognition. The results of the analyses are deemed *preliminary* because of the uncertainty of any estimates (see Appendix 1 for further discussion; Re: *explosive uncertainty* and *estimation error*; elusiveness of "true" distributions; *meta-uncertainty* and *meta-probability*).

Data. The data consists of annual financial data of a single non-financial firm in the consumer goods sector that operates in all geographic regions (worldwide). The firm's estimated market capitalization by then end of 2017 was approximately $U.S. 200 billion. For further details on the data and the key variables studied, see Appendix 1.

A. Estimation of CNRI with Historical Data

The previous discussion of interest rates (credit-based and firm-specific natural interest rates) used a deterministic approach to *equity income* where the SOR was fixed at 25 in the simple examples provided.

The variables are not fixed and from this point, the analysis attempts to consider random fluctuations in the variable. The key variable to be examined is RRC as the theoretical upper limit as well as an indicator of *opportunity cost*.

The fitted probability distribution of RRC allows us to *estimate* the probability that RRC would fall below (or above) a given value of RRC. (*) The term "estimate" must account for *estimation error* which the next section hopes to address.

10-Year Sets, Sequential. Because the term and amortization of the hypothetical loan is 10 years, the credit-based natural interest rate also must correspond to the same time period, 10 years. Therefore, the annual historical observations of the variable RRC are divided into *sets* of 10 years each, in sequence such that each set is shifted by one year. Each set is labelled, such as Set 1, Set 2, etc. For example, Set 1 is the 10-year set from 2007-2016, Set 2 is the 10-year set shifted by one year 2015-2006, and so on. For further detail, see Appendix 1 regarding distribution fitting of the observations. Charts of the relative frequency distributions of these 10-year sets for all variables are also shown in Appendix 3 to give a dynamic "moving" picture of the variables.

Probability Scenarios
Refer to the **RRC Scenarios** table below of probabilities and corresponding values for RRC. When calculating probabilities, a given point is specified as a *delimiter* denoted as X_1. Then, the probability is estimated that the random variable X (which here is RRC) would be *less than* X_1, or $P(X<X_1)$.

Table: RRC Probability Scenarios: Left (0.05, 0.10), Center (0.50)

#	Specified Probability (P)	X_1 for Entire Dataset*	X_1 Set 1 (2016-2007)	X_1 Set 2 (2015-2006)
1	$P(X<X_1)=0.05, P(X>X_1)=0.95$	0.026	0.026	0.010
2	$P(X<X_1)=0.10, P(X>X_1)=0.90$	0.047	0.095	0.096
3	$P(X<X_1)=0.5, P(X>X_1)=0.5$	0.143	0.160	0.179
	Fitted Distribution (pdf)	Johnson SB	Cauchy	Cauchy

(*)Entire Dataset: 2016-1988.

For brevity, the above table presents just three of the 20 fitted datasets as follows (by column):
1. X_1 **Entire dataset** 2016-1988 (also called "ALL")
2. X_1 **Set 1**: The 10-year period 2016-2007

40

3. X_1 **Set 2**: The 10-year period 2015-2006

In **Scenario (row) #1**, the cell in the column titled "X_1 for Entire Dataset" shows a value of 0.026. This value indicates that when RRC is 0.026 (this value for RRC is the delimiter X_1), then the probability that RRC<0.026 is 0.05; the probability that RRC>0.026 is (1-.05) =0.95. Note that RRC<0.026 is in the *left tail* of the distribution.

Scenarios #1 and #2 focus on the *left tail* where $P(X<X_1)$ is 0.05 or 0.10, respectively.

Example of Scenario #2. The following chart is of the estimated CNRI for **Scenario #2**, the left tail scenario where P=0.10, $P(X<X_1)$. The chart is repeated later below alongside historical 10-year bond yields for purposes of comparison. This scenario may also be abbreviated as the "left tail P=0.10 scenario," P=0.10 or as P=10%.

CNRI Range. In the charts there is a range for the CNRI which reflects an arbitrary 2% margin implied for the borrower defining a theoretical upper limit and lower limit for the CNRI It should be clarified that if the borrower can obtain a rate below the lower limit, it will likely do so.

If the upper limit of the RRC at P=0.10, $P(X<X_1)$ is 9.5%, then the lower limit is arbitrarily assumed to be 9.5%-2%=7.5%. It is considered likely that the borrower would consider a rate of 6% if offered, although 6% may not be acceptable to the lender subject to the opportunity cost of the lender (i.e. what return could be earned elsewhere); nevertheless, this range is only a rough indicator. The chart below shows the CNRI range for RRC at P=0.10, $P(X<X_1)$:

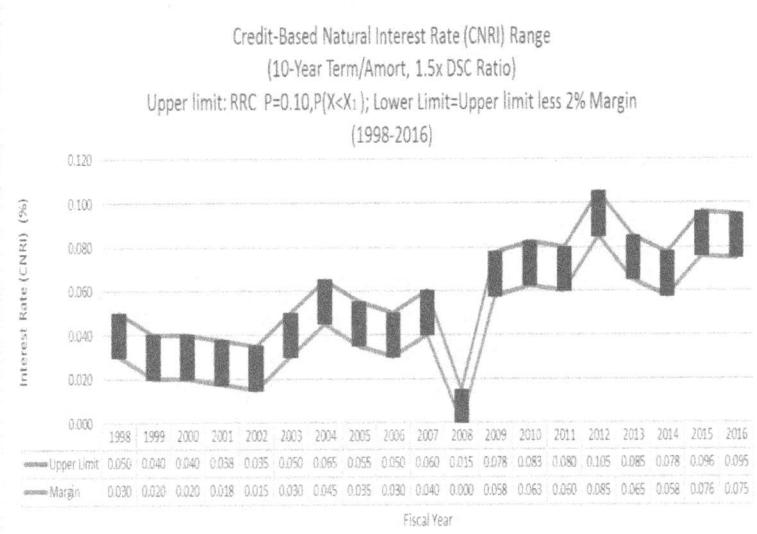

Credit-Based Natural Interest Rate (CNRI) Range
(10-Year Term/Amort, 1.5x DSC Ratio)
Upper limit: RRC P=0.10,P(X<X₁); Lower Limit=Upper limit less 2% Margin
(1998-2016)

Fiscal Year	1998	1999	2000	2001	2002	2003	2004	2005	2006	2007	2008	2009	2010	2011	2012	2013	2014	2015	2016
Upper Limit	0.050	0.040	0.040	0.038	0.035	0.050	0.065	0.055	0.050	0.060	0.015	0.078	0.083	0.080	0.105	0.085	0.078	0.096	0.095
Margin	0.030	0.020	0.020	0.018	0.015	0.030	0.045	0.035	0.030	0.040	0.000	0.058	0.063	0.060	0.085	0.065	0.058	0.076	0.075

Scenario #3 is the "center scenario" [P=0.50, P(X<X₁) or P(X>X₁)] in which the probability is equal to 0.50 (or 50%) on *both* sides of the given point X_1. For example, in row #3, the cell with the value 0.143 is the value of RRC (this is the X_1) when both P(X<X₁) and P(X>X₁) =0.5. The importance of this scenario will be detailed in the next section.

Fitted Distributions for RRC
The fitted distributions and parameter estimates for RRC for each of the datasets shown in the last row of the table above are as follows:
1. **Entire Dataset**: Johnson SB (0.499; 2.18; 0.669; -0.15475).
2. **Set 1** (10 years) 2016-2007 Cauchy (0.02118; 0.15994), ranked #1 for the K-S, A-D, and Chi-Squared tests.
3. **Set 2** (10 years) 2015-2006 Cauchy (0.02696; 0.17902) also top-ranked for the K-S and A-D tests (Chi-Squared n/a).

Radar Charts. The radar chart below shows the fitted sets in a clockwise order, beginning with the *entire dataset* ("ALL") at the top the 12 o'clock position, followed at right by Set 1 (2016-2007),

Set 2 (2015-2006), and so on. Had all the fitted distributions been identical, the radar chart would trace a circle.

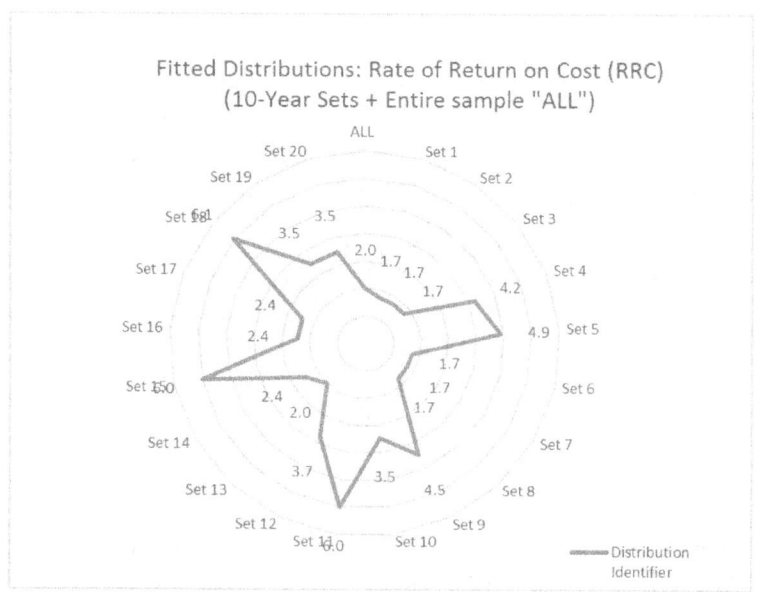

Relative Frequency of Distributions. The top three relatively most frequent fitted distributions are shown in the following table. The Cauchy distribution (Identifier: 1.7) comprises 29% of the total fitted distributions. The right column titled "identifier" refers to the numeric code given for the distribution.

Name	Rel. Freq	Identifier
Cauchy	0.29	1.7
Error	0.14	2.4
GEV	0.14	3.5

Notes: The term "Error" in the above table refers to the *name* of the distribution, not error as in *standard error* or *estimation error* (see next section). GEV refers to the generalized extreme value distribution. (For further detail on distribution-fitting, see Appendix 1)

The CNRI and Accounting for Estimation Error

What value best represents the "true" value for the upper limit? In truth, any such value is essentially unknowable. At best, allowing for an exceedingly *high estimation error* is *essential* given the small samples of this study, imprecision, and given the likelihood that we not necessarily dealing with underlying Gaussian environments (see caveats in the Notes of this section, particularly comments by Taleb; for details on fitted distributions of the variables of this study, see Appendix 1).

As an attempt to address these issues, **Scenario #3**, the "Center Scenario" where P=0.50, $P(X<X_1)$ or $P(X>X_1)$, is introduced based on a concept of maximum ignorance (Re: Laplace's Law of Error): When confronted with many observations of the same event—the "true" value would be equally likely to be located above or below the center (i.e. *milieu de probabilité*), or the *center of error* (*milieu d'erreur* or *milieu astronomique*) where the sum of the absolute errors multiplied by their probabilities is a minimum (Laplace 1774, 1781, 1786; also see Taleb 2012: 447-455, Gorroochum, 2016). Therefore, **Scenario #3** is intended to encompass a sufficiently massive estimation error to obtain a better measure of natural rates of return.

*Notes and Caveats: 1. Per a *taxonomy of ignorance* (Smithson 1989) the term *ignorance* and *uncertainty* can be treated nearly synonymously although uncertainty is a subcategory of, and viewed as a narrower concept than ignorance. Uncertainty is also a subcategory of *error* (Smithson 1989:9).

2. Concepts of *explosive uncertainty* (error) and non-computability: Regarding *Knightian uncertainty* (Knight 1928) see Taleb (2012:455); a critical concern is uncertainty due to *minute imprecisions* in parameter estimation itself ("estimation implies error") even given *normal* distributions; the problem worsens with fat tails: "...*all tails* are uncertain under the slightest perturbation and their effect is severe in fat-tailed domains, that is economic life." "...fat tails mean incomputability of tail events, little else." (455). Also note in *nonparametric* derivation of probabilities as the probability approaches 1/sample size, the error also explodes (454). Also re: concepts of *meta-uncertainty* and *meta-probability*.

Returning to the RRC Scenarios table above, in Scenario #3 and the column for Set 1 (the 10-year period 2016-2007), the probability that RRC would fall below (or above) 0.16 (16%) is 0.50 (fitted distribution: Cauchy). This does not imply that 0.16 (or 16%) represents an estimate of any final agreed-upon interest rate for a qualifying loan, only that it represents a theoretical *upper limit* to the borrower; this should incorporate *randomness* of the rate of return (RRC) as well as potential for massive error. Also recall that the final interest rate will depend upon negotiation in the loanable funds market and cannot be known until undistorted market rates of interest are permitted to exist. It is likely that any negotiated rate would be significantly lower in this scenario.

Nevertheless, for the lender, greater uncertainty of the environment (firm, industry, economic, political, etc.), can cause *required returns* to rise to compensate for the uncertainty, putting upward pressure on the CNRI. This in turn would have a "braking effect" on the amount of loanable funds that lenders may be willing to commit without commanding a higher interest rate. This is seen as a natural, self-regulating mechanism.

Credit-based Natural Interest Rates (CNRIs):
Estimates vs. 10-Year Bond Rates

The CNRIs are presented in the order of the three scenarios in the table titled "**RRC Scenarios: Left (0.05, 0.10) and Center (0.50)**" above. Estimates are for the period 1998-2016 for hypothetical 10-year loans and are charted alongside historical U.S. Treasury 10-year bond yields. The fitted distributions are for the 10-year sets*. In arbitrary profit margin of 2% is inserted which creates a "band" below the upper limit of the RRC; the borrower is expected to negotiate below this upper limit as explained above.

*See Appendix 1 for further detail on distribution fitting.

CNRI Scenario #1: Left Tail [P=0.05, P(X<X_1)]

The left tail is an area of the distribution that corresponds to *lower* returns. The CNRIs estimated in this scenario for a hypothetical 10-year term loan (based on the upper limit of the firm's natural return) and historical 10-year bond yields are shown in the chart below:

(This scenario may also be abbreviated as the "left tail P=0.05 scenario" or as P=5%)

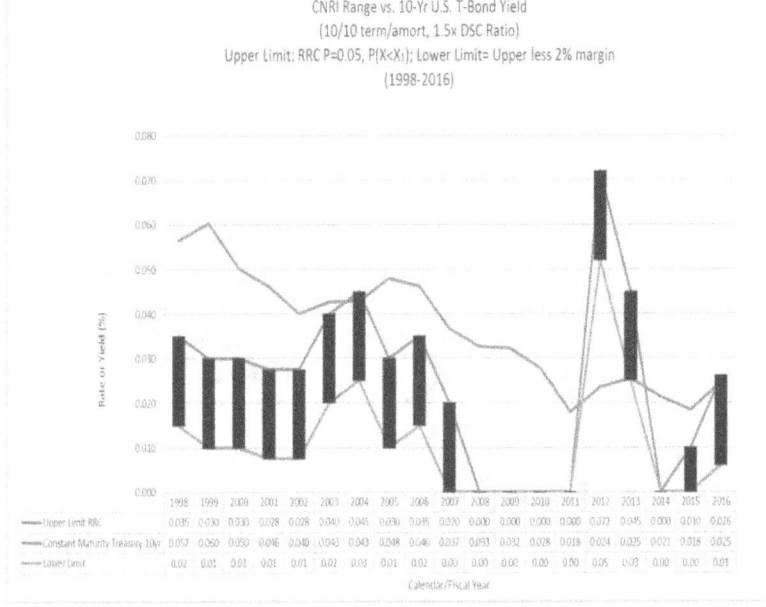

Source of bond data: Board of Governors of the Federal Reserve System (US), 10-Year Treasury Constant Maturity Rate (Series ID: DGS10, Release: *H.15 Selected Interest Rates*).

Interpretation: If the firm-specific natural rate of return (as represented by RRC) and corresponding CNRI for the firm are assumed to be in the left tail at [P=0.05, $P(X<X_1)$] of each distribution, there may be some rough similarity in trend between actual historical 10-year bond yields and these estimates for hypothetical 10-year loan rates.

CNRI Scenario #2: Left Tail [P=0.10, $P(X<X_1)$]
In this case the returns encompass a *higher* range within the left tail than in **Scenario #1**. The CNRIs estimated in this scenario for a hypothetical 10-year term loan (based on the upper limit of the firm's natural return) and historical 10-year bond yields are shown in the chart below:

46

(This scenario may also be abbreviated as the "left tail P=0.10 scenario" or as P=10%).

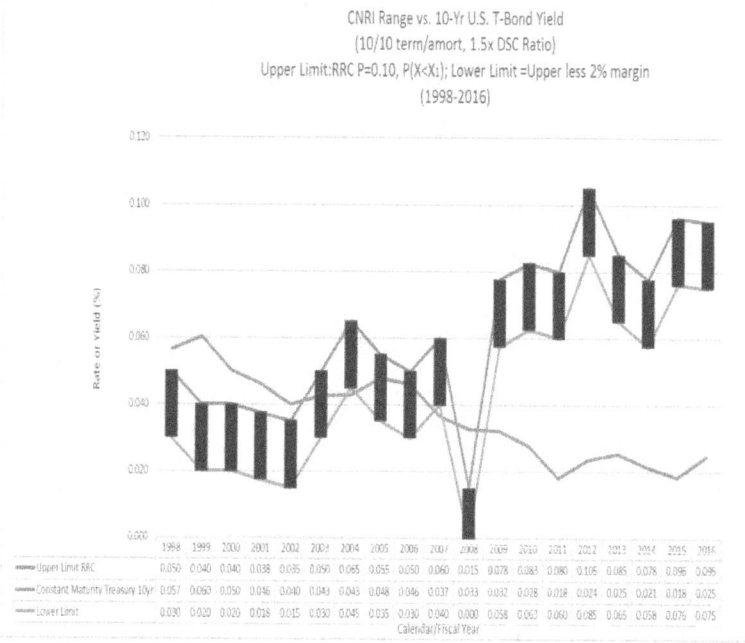

CNRI Range vs. 10-Yr U.S. T-Bond Yield
(10/10 term/amort, 1.5x DSC Ratio)
Upper Limit:RRC P=0.10, P(X<X₁); Lower Limit =Upper less 2% margin
(1998-2016)

	1998	1999	2000	2001	2002	2003	2004	2005	2006	2007	2008	2009	2010	2011	2012	2013	2014	2015	2016
Upper Limit RRC	0.050	0.040	0.040	0.038	0.035	0.050	0.065	0.065	0.050	0.060	0.015	0.078	0.083	0.080	0.105	0.085	0.078	0.096	0.095
Constant Maturity Treasury 10yr	0.057	0.060	0.050	0.046	0.040	0.043	0.043	0.048	0.046	0.037	0.033	0.032	0.078	0.018	0.024	0.025	0.021	0.018	0.025
Lower Limit	0.030	0.020	0.020	0.018	0.015	0.030	0.045	0.035	0.030	0.040	0.000	0.058	0.063	0.060	0.085	0.065	0.058	0.076	0.075

Calendar/Fiscal Year

Interpretation: If the firm-specific natural rate of return and corresponding CNRI for the firm are set in the left tail at [P=0.010, P(X<X₁)] of each distribution, there is now a significant departure between the historical 10-year bond yields and the estimates for the hypothetical 10-year loan rates, *particularly after 2008* where bond yields continued downward.

CNRI Scenario #3: Center [P=0.50, P(X<X₁) or P(X>X₁)].
The center is an area of the distribution that corresponds to a theoretical midpoint of returns where error is assumed to be at maximum (as discussed above in accounting for estimation error). This case assumes that the returns encompass a higher range (i.e. 50%) than in both **Scenario #1 and Scenario #2** above. The CNRIs estimated in this scenario for a hypothetical 10-year term

loan (based on the upper limit of the firm's natural return) and historical 10-year bond yields are shown in the chart below: *(This scenario may also be abbreviated as the "center P=0.50 scenario" or as P=50%.)*

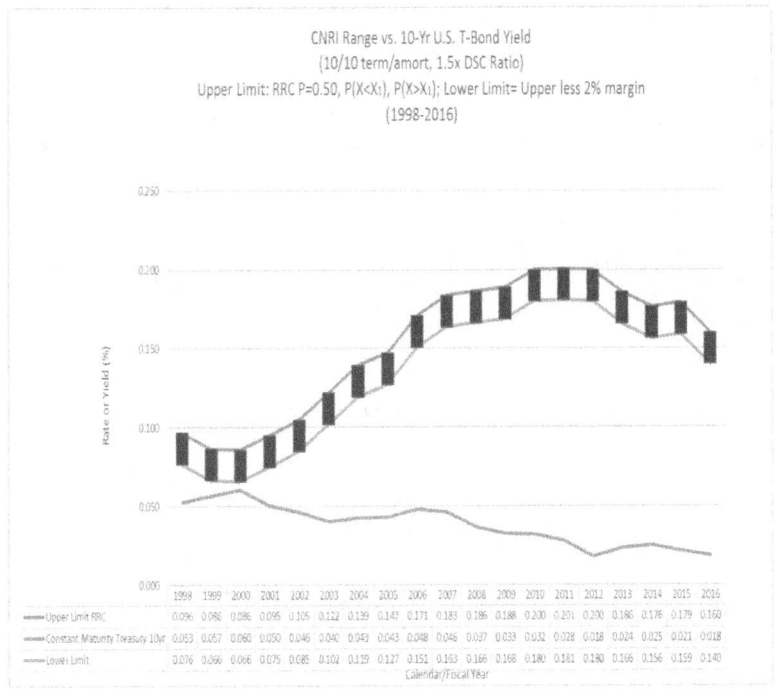

Interpretation: If the firm-specific natural rate of return and corresponding CNRI for the firm are assumed to be situated in the *center* of each distribution at $[P=0.50, P(X<X_1), P(X>X_1)]$, compared to the previous scenarios there is an even greater departure between the historical 10-year bond yields and the estimates for hypothetical 10-year loan rates; this divergence begins earlier as well, in 2000, after which actual bond yields have seen an overall downward trend.

B. Evidence of Financial Distortion: Asset Mispricing

B.1. Asset Mispricing: Debt

In Part I we saw a historical chart of the *riskfree* rate which can be viewed as reflecting policy interest rates for 90-day maturities.

The inverse relationship between the present value of assets and the discount rate also was shown to suggest that the trend of declining policy interest rates may have contributed to asset price inflation which are likely to encompass the values of both debt and equity securities.

Moreover, a declining trend of policy interest rates might be expected to take on more debt than would have been the case without this distortion in borrowing costs. Financial data for the consumer goods firm of this study are shown below, beginning with the history of total liabilities as a percentage of revenues:

Debt Accumulation History (1990-2016)

A trend line is added to indicate a rough trajectory. Note that the total liabilities data for 1991was not obtainable and therefore a value was interpolated between 1992 and 1990; this should not materially affect the overall trend.

Credit-Based Interest Rate (CBI) (Existing Debt) Estimates
The credit-based interest rate (CBI) is computed based on a hypothetical refinance of existing debt loads in each fiscal year. Refer to the chart below:

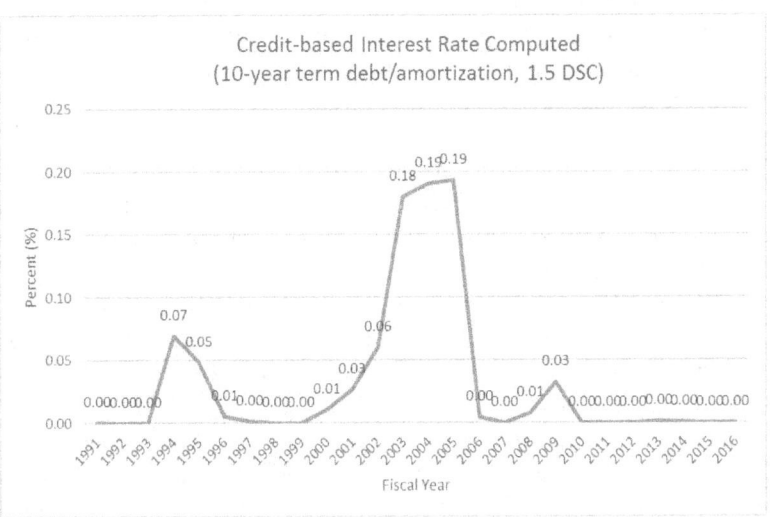

The spike from approx. 2002 to 2007 was due to the combination of a lowered debt load (relative to revenues), and an elevated source of repayment (SOR) during that period.

The elevated CBIs as seen in the chart does not suggest that the firm would ever have paid such a rate. Rather, the firm would have been capable of handling a greater debt load at that time due to improved debt service capacity. Recall that the computed CBI must decline to make the refinanced loan more "affordable" when there is more debt relative to the source of repayment (SOR). Recall that a *zero* CBI indicates that the firm cannot service a refinancing of its existing debt load given the assumptions (see below under "amount of refinance."

As noted elsewhere, interest rates should be seen in a longer-term context; outstanding cash flow and debt service capacity for a few years is viewed as insufficient from a term lending perspective.

50

Amount of Refinance. The refinance amount is hypothetical as it is arbitrarily assumed to equal to 50% of the total liabilities/revenues ratio. Therefore, if in 2015 the TL/Revs ratio was 1.45 then the refinance amount is 1.45/2 or .725 of revenues.

To clarify, the hypothetical amount of refinance is a simple tool of analysis and may not represent the *actual* debt service amount as per the company financial statements. * Business debt service reflects a multitude of different types of loans with varying interest rates and repayment schedules.

*Note: There can be variations on the measure of actual debt service. For example, debt service could be defined as the sum of current (or most recent) interest expense/finance charges plus the current portion of long-term debt (CPLTD. Alternatively, it might be more appropriate to refer to the annual (future) maturities of long-term debt, coupled with the current interest expense/finance charges; preparing a schedule based on future *averages* of maturities may be inappropriate because the debt must be entirely serviced in each year and averages may underrepresent the amount of debt service required.

Terms of Refinance. The terms of the debt refinance are always assumed to be a 10-year term with matching amortization (=10/10) and 1.5x debt service coverage ratio.

B.2. Asset Mispricing: Equities

Stock Price and Rates of Return (RRC)
When prices or costs diverge from some measure(s) of fundamental value, presence of a distortion in the form of asset mispricing is viewed as more likely. In Kennedy (2016), asset mispricing was theorized to occur when asset prices diverge from a fundamental defined as a rate of return measure called the *rate of return on cost* (RRC). *Over/undervaluation* of an asset is believed to occur when prices of the assets increase/decrease relative to fundamentals such as RRC or RRCG. For more detail on fundamentals and pricing, see Appendix 2. In this section, various forms of analysis are conducted to identify overvaluation or undervaluation of stock prices relative to rates of return on cost (RRC) based on historical data of a consumer goods firm.

Regression Analysis. If some relationship is assumed between two variables, a method such as *regression analysis* can be used to show possible evidence of the relationship, with caveats. *Linearity* is assumed although real-world variables are expected to be non-linear. The estimation method is simple *ordinary least squares* (OLS); shortcomings of regression analysis, of which there are many, are detailed further in Appendix 2.

The results of the analysis are shown here, comparing an asset price variable, stock price changes (SPG) to (1) the *actual* annual rate of return on cost (RRC) and (2) annual *changes* in the RRC (RRCG). The letter "G" indicates annual *changes* ("G" for "growth") in these variables; ACT refers to *actual*, SP is stock price, and FREQ is an abbreviation for *relative frequency*.

The data are for the *entire sample* of each variable with observations from 1990-2016; for details on the data, variables, and datasets, see Appendix 1.

Relationship Between Stock Price and Returns. A regression estimate (OLS) suggests a positive and significant relationship between changes in stock prices (SPG) and changes in the firm's rate of return (RRC):

$$SPGFREQ = 0.014 + 0.71 RRCGFREQ$$
$$(1.21)\,(4.1)$$
$$Radj = .43 \quad F = 16.8$$

However, this is considered invalid because the observations are relative frequency distributions, of which many values are zero for both variables, which considerably improves the correlation. Therefore, an alternative regression estimate employed only one zero on each tail. The results suggest a much weaker positive relationship:

$$SPGFREQ = 0.031 + 0.535 RRCGFREQ$$
$$(1.49)\,(2.23)$$
$$Radj = .22 \quad F = 5.0$$

Interestingly, similar, and slightly improved results were obtained for the estimate between changes in the stock price and *the actual* annual RRC values (not *changes* in the RRC).

$$SPGFREQ = 0.027 + 0.36 RRCGFREQ$$
$$(2.36)\,(2.89)$$
$$Radj = .26 \quad F = 8.4$$

It should also be clarified that the significance of the equation's *constant* was weak enough to cast doubt on the overall significance of these weak relationships. In conclusion, significant correlation between the variables does not seem to be definitive.

Relative Frequency Distributions. Histograms graphing the relative frequency distributions for variables SPG and RRCG are shown here with an overlay of the fitted distribution (see Appendix 1 for details on variables and distribution fitting):

Change in Stock Price (SPG)

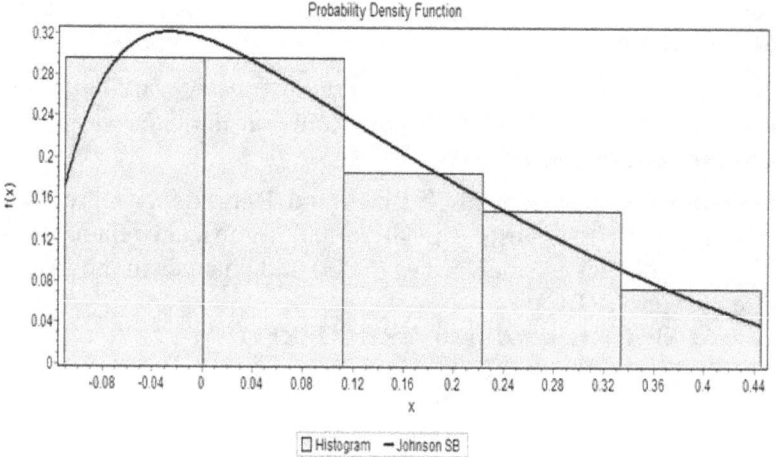

Change in Rate of Return on Cost (RRCG)

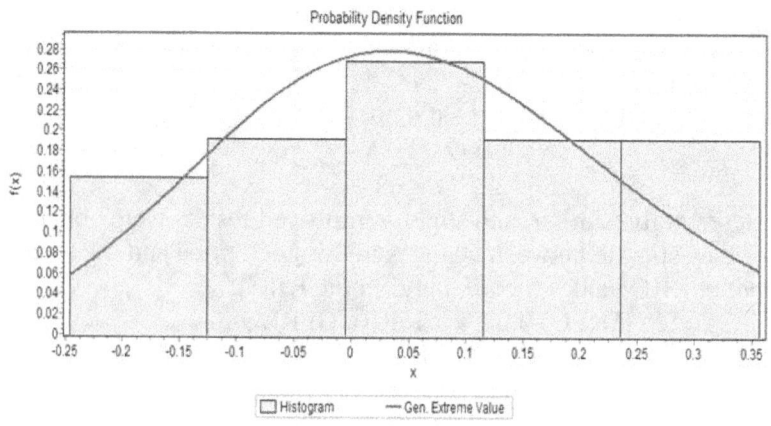

Histograms graphing relative frequency distributions with fitted distribution overlay are also shown below for the other three variables of the study: *Equity income* (as a percentage of revenues, EI%), *rate of return on cost* (RRC), and *change in revenues* (REVG). See Appendix 1 and 2 for further detail on distribution fitting and background on the variables.

Equity Income (EI%)

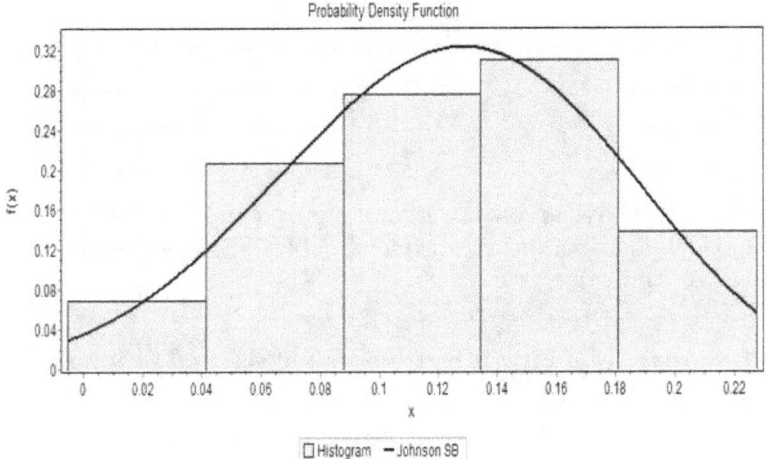

Rate of Return on Cost (RRC)

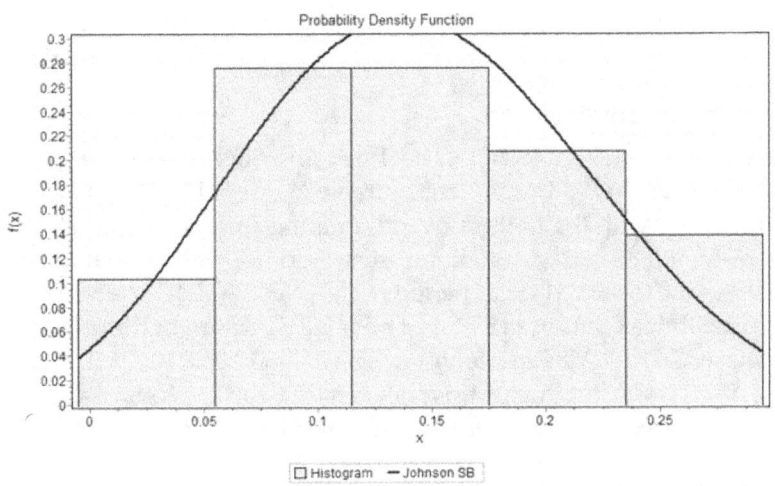

Change in Revenues, Annual (REVG)

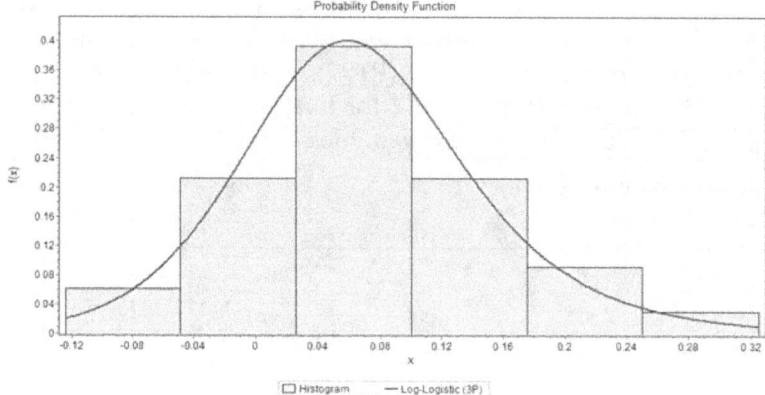

Note: For a dynamic view ("moving" picture) of the relative frequency distributions of all five variables in sequential 10-year sets, see Appendix 3.

Ratio Analysis of Fitted Distribution for Selected Probabilities (Radar Charts)

This section is supplemented by Appendix 1 on fitted distributions.

Variables and Methodology

To obtain another measure of over/undervaluation, the variables compared are *annual changes in the stock price* (SPG, where "G" refers to growth), and *annual changes in the rate of return on cost* (RRCG).

Fitted Distributions

RRC Changes (RRCG). The fitted distribution for the entire dataset (2016-1988) was Gen. Extreme Value (-0.22606; 0.16346; -0.00836) with the highest overall ranking for the K-S, A-D, and Chi-Squared tests. In addition, distributions were fitted for the variable for each 10-year period (Set 1, Set 2, etc.)

Stock Price Changes (SPG). The fitted distribution for the entire dataset 2016-1988 was Johnson SB (0.84538; 0.94002; 0.75005; -0.1452) with the highest overall ranking for the K-S, A-D, and Chi-Squared tests. In addition, distributions were fitted for the variable for each 10-year period (Set 1, Set 2, etc.).

Probabilities and Corresponding Data Points. The table below shows the data points that correspond to the probability of 95%, based on the fitted distribution for the *entire dataset* (data points for the 10-year sets are not shown in this table).

Variable and Ratio	Probability	Entire Dataset
RRC Changes (RRCG)	P=0.95	0.35
Stock P Changes (SPG)	P=0.95	0.38
Ratio (SPG/RRCG)		1.10

Entire dataset is for 1988-2016

RRCG. For the entire dataset (1988-2016) and its fitted distribution, the point 0.35 corresponds to a probability of 0.95, which means that the probability of RRCG falling *below* the point 0.35 is 95% (and *above* the point 0.35 the probability is 5%*). This also can be written as $P(X<X_1) =0.95$ where X_1 is the data point* for RRCG of 0.35.

*Notes: What is called the *data point* here, or X_1, can also be referred to as the *delimiter* since it is the point below which we wish to estimate the probability. Since the difference between 1 (=100% probability) and 0.95 is 0.05, for $P(X>X_1)$, the same data point X_1 of 0.35 has a probability of 0.05.

SPG. For the entire dataset (1988-2016) and fitted distribution, the point 0.38 corresponds to a probability of 0.95, which means that the probability of SPG falling below the point 0.38 is 95% (and *above* the point 0.38 the probability is 5%). This also can be written as $P(X<X_1) =0.95$ where X_1 is the delimiter for RRCG of 0.38.

Ratio (SPG/RRCG). As can be seen from the table above, the data points that correspond to P=0.95 for RRCG and SPG are 0.35 and 0.38, respectively. The ratio SPG/RRCG yields a value of 1.10.

Valuation and Evidence of Mispricing

Does the ratio computed above suggest overvaluation or undervaluation? To begin, the assumptions of over/undervaluation are summarized:

Assumptions

Variables and (Over/Under) valuation Ratio. The two underlying variables are: RRCG, the change in rate of return on cost, and SPG, the change in the stock price. The value corresponding to a specified *probability* is based on the fitted distribution for each 10-year period for each variable. Because there are two variables, the ratio compares the probabilities for each of the *two* distributions.

Each of these 10-year periods is referred to as a "Set"; the entire dataset of all observations is abbreviated as "ALL", covering the period 2016 to 1988. These 10-year periods are sequential, each shifted by one year (e.g. Set 1 2016-2007, Set 2 2015-2006, etc.).

Fundamentals. Recall from Kennedy (2016) that RRC is assumed to be a fundamental source of value of the stock, *changes* in RRC, which are expressed by the variable RRCG, are therefore assumed to be changes in the underlying "fundamental" value of the stock. See Appendix 2 for additional discussion on fundamentals.

Subdividing the Distribution. An attempt is made to arbitrarily "split up" the fitted distributions into three basic sections where the observations may lie; the probabilities P=0.05, P=0.5, and P=0.95 were selected. The reasoning behind subdividing the distribution is that valuations and departure from fundamentals may differ between the extremes (left and right tail), and the extremes may also differ from the central area (where the bulk of the data are assumed to occur).

Abbreviations. The *right tail* may be abbreviated as "right tail P=0.95," the *left tail* as "left tail P=0.05" and the *center* abbreviated as P=0.5. These abbreviations must be clarified. In all scenarios what is of primary interest is the value *below* which the estimated probability of the variable is the specified probability, or $P(X<X_1)$. To avoid confusion, the abbreviated "right tail P=0.95" might better be written as [P=0.95, $P(X<X_1)$, P=0.05, $P(X>X_1)$], the *left tail* P=0.05 as [(P=0.05, $P(X<X_1)$], and the *center* as [P=0.50, for $P(X<X_1)$, $P(X>X_1)$].

We begin with the right tail scenario below explaining the steps in more detail.

Summary Findings in Tables

Right Tail Scenario [P=0.95, P(X<X₁) or P=0.05, P(X>X₁)].
Refer to the table below for an explanation of the steps involved in the computations. **Row #1** for RRCG shows a value of 0.345 under the column titled "Entire Dataset." This 0.345 is the value of RRCG *below which* the probability of RRCG occurring is 0.95 (or 95%), also written as $P(X<X_1)$ =0.95; the remaining 5% is *above* the value of 0.345 is (1-0.95) =0.05 and is located in the *right tail* of that distribution.

In **row #2**, the same-period value for the second variable, SPG, is 0.38 which is the value of SPG below which the probability of RRCG occurring is 0.95 (or 95%).

Row #3 shows the ratio SPG/RRCG and is 1.10 because the value of the stock price changes at the *same* probability of 95% tends to be higher than the value of the changes in changes in the rate of return (0.38 versus 0.345).

Right Tail Scenario [P=0.95, P(X<X1) or P=0.05, P(X>X1)]				
#	Variables and Ratio	Specified Probability (P)	X₁ for Entire Dataset (2016-1988)	X₁ Set 1 (2016-2007)
1	RRC Changes (RRCG)	P(X<X₁)=0.95	0.345	0.1296
2	Stock Price Changes (SPG)	P(X<X₁)=0.95	0.38	0.16309
3	Ratio (SPG/ RRCG)	P(X<X₁)=0.95, both variables	1.10	1.26
4	Fitted Distributions (pdf)	RRCG	Gen Extreme Val.	Johnson SB
		SPG	Johnson SB	Gen Extreme Val

Note: X₁ is the variable's *delimiter*--the value below which the estimated P of that variable is 0.95.

If the ratio exceeds 1 in the *right tail*, the result is assumed to be an *overvaluation*. This is because for the *same* probability of occurrence, the stock price change (SPG) exceeds the fundamentals as represented by the change in the rate of return (RRCG). Looking at the results, the ratio of 1.26 for the second data column (covering Set 1for the 10-year period from 2016-2007) exceeds the ratio of 1.10 for the entire datasets which cover the period from 2016-1988. This suggests greater *recent* overvaluation relative to the historical record.

In the table, the section labelled **#4 Fitted Distributions** shows the fitted distributions (*probability density functions* or pdf) for each variable's dataset: The Generalized Extreme Value and Johnson SB were evaluated as the best-fitting distributions due to the highest ranks in testing. For more detail on distribution fitting see Appendix 1.

Left Tail Scenario (P=0.05, P(X<X_1).) If the ratio is *less than* 1 in the left tail, the result is viewed as an *overvaluation*. This is because for the *same* probability, SPG changes *less* than the RRCG, suggesting that the decline in the assumed fundamental source of value, RRC, is *not fully reflected* in the stock price – in other words the stock price remains "sticky" to the upside despite the deteriorating fundamentals.

For example, in the table below, for the period 1988-2016 (entire dataset), for a left tail probability of 0.05, the corresponding data point is -0.21 (*negative* 21% or a 21% decline in RRCG); this means that the probability of RRCG falling below negative 0.21 is estimated at 5%. As for stock price changes (SPG), the corresponding data point at the same probability of 0.05 is only -**0.10** (negative 0.10), which is *less* of a decline than RRCG, leading to a ratio well under 1, of 0.453. The results for the P=0.05 left tail scenario are presented in the table below.

Left Tail Scenario [P=0.05, P(X<X1)]				
#	Variables and Ratio	Specified Probability (P)	X1 for Entire Dataset (2016-1988)	X1 Set 1 (2016-2007)
1	RRC Changes (RRCG)	P(X<X1)=0.05	-0.212	-0.26742
2	Stock Price Changes (SPG)	P(X<X1)=0.05	-0.096	-0.01968
3	**Ratio (SPG/ RRCG)**	P(X<X1)=0.05, both variables	**0.45**	**0.07**
4	**Fitted Distributions (pdf)**	RRCG	Gen Extreme Val.	Johnson SB
		SPG	Johnson SB	Gen Extreme Val

Note: X1 is the variable's *delimiter*--the value below which the estimated P of that variable is 0.05.

Center Scenario [P=0.50, for P(X<X_1), P(X>X_1)], an overvaluation is assumed to occur when the ratio exceeds 1. In the table below, the data points corresponding to a probability of

0.50 are shown for RRCG and SPG. The ratio of 1.46 suggests that for the same probability, stock price changes tend to be greater than changes in the fundamentals (RRCG).

Center Scenario [P=0.50, P(X<X1), P(X>X1)]				
#	Variables and Ratio	Specified Probability (P)	X1 for Entire Dataset (2016-1988)	X1 Set 1 (2016-2007)
1	RRC Changes (RRCG)	P(X<X1)=0.50	0.04914	0.0004915
2	Stock Price Changes (SPG)	P(X<X1)=0.50	0.07171	0.08235
3	Ratio (SPG/ RRCG)	P(X<X1)=0.50, both variables	1.46	167.55
4	Fitted Distributions (pdf)	RRCG	Gen Extreme Val.	Johnson SB
		SPG	Johnson SB	Gen Extreme Val

Note: X1 is the variable's *delimiter*, the value below/above which the estimated P of that variable is 0.50.

Special Note: Outliers. In row #3, the Set 1 column, note the elevated ratio of 167.55. It is recognized that the reasons for an outlier should be examined before attempting to remove or substitute for the outlier. In this case, the ratio resulted because of an apparent 50% probability of a *near-zero change* in RRCG during the 10-year period 2016-2007 (Set 1). The topic of possible *outliers* is addressed further in the discussion below.

Summary of Overall Valuation Results
The results from all three scenarios above are shown in the next table, along with the results for two other scenarios: P=0.10, P(X<X1), and [P=0.90 P(X<X1) or P=0.10 P(X>X1)]. An additional 10-year period set (Set 2 for 2015-2006) is shown. In sum, an overall pattern of overvaluation appears to be the norm.

Valuation Summary				
Overvaluation Case (Ratio)	Specified Probability (P)	Entire Dataset	Set 1 (2016-2007)	Set 2 (2015-2006)
(SPG/ RRCG)>1	P(X<X1)=0.95, both variables	1.10	1.26	1.11
(SPG/ RRCG)>1	P(X<X1)=0.90, both variables	1.13	1.24	1.07
(SPG/ RRCG)<1	P(X<X1)=0.05, both variables	0.45	0.07	0.23
(SPG/ RRCG)<1	P(X<X1)=0.10, both variables	0.47	0.01	0.21
(SPG/ RRCG)>1	P(X<X1)=0.50, both variables	1.46	1.68	1.10

Entire dataset (1988-2016); other periods are 10-year sets.

X_1 is the variable's *delimiter*--the value below which the estimated P of that variable is the specified probability.

Summary Findings in Radar Charts

The computed ratios of over/undervaluation are now presented in a radar chart format which gives a full view of each 10-year period (referred to as Sets) as well as for the entire dataset (referred to as "ALL"). The chart runs clockwise, from Set 1 to Set 14: Set 1 is the most recent 10-year period 2016-2007, Set 2 is 2015-2006, continuing until the earliest period (Set 14) which is 2003-1994.

Theoretical "Perfect" Valuation Scenario. A theoretical "perfect" alignment between price and fundamentals in a radar chart would be described by a ratio of 1 for every 10-year period as well as for the entire dataset ("ALL" located in the 12 o'clock position at top). This alignment case would appear as a circle as in the diagram below:

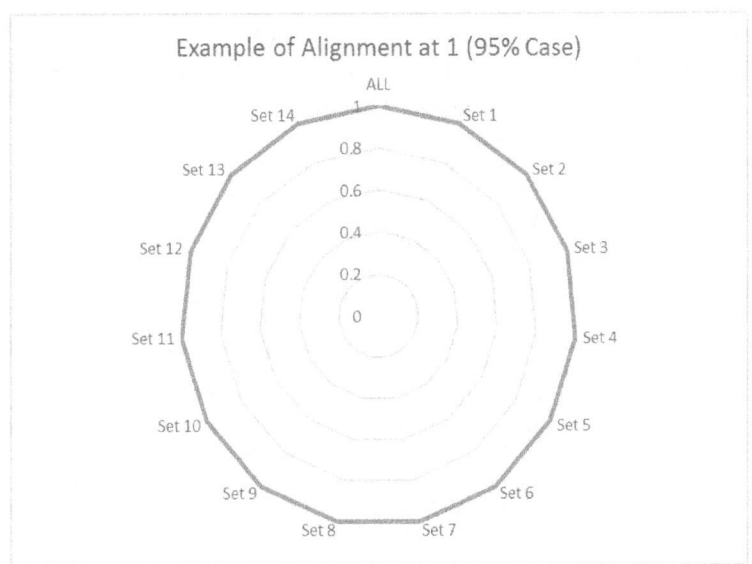

Example of Alignment at 1 (95% Case)

This chart is only presented for comparison purposes and is not intended to reflect reality. The results of the computed ratios based on historical data are shown below.

Notes on Outliers

A challenge of working with data is the presence of so-called *outliers* which in fact are may *not* be outliers and should not necessarily be removed from the datasets. Of the 75 computed ratios, there were three data points treated as outliers: In the right tail [P=0.95, $P(X<X_1)$ or P=0.05, $P(X>X_1)$], scenario, Set 12 was found to be a significant outlier; in the central (P=0.50) case, both Set 1 and 2 were thought to be major outliers.

Detail

Right Tail Scenario. In the right tail [P=0.95, $P(X<X_1)$ or P=0.05, $P(X>X_1)$], one outlier was observed for **Set 12** (2005-1996). In that sample period, RRCG was .345, SPG was 1.06 and the ratio of SPG/RRCG was 3.1. The ratio for Set 12 is significantly greater than the ratio of 1.1 computed for the entire dataset (2016-1988).

For purposes of illustration, the *unadjusted* right tail P=0.95 scenario is shown in the radar chart below (unadjusted Set 12 corresponding to the 10-year period 2005 to 1996).

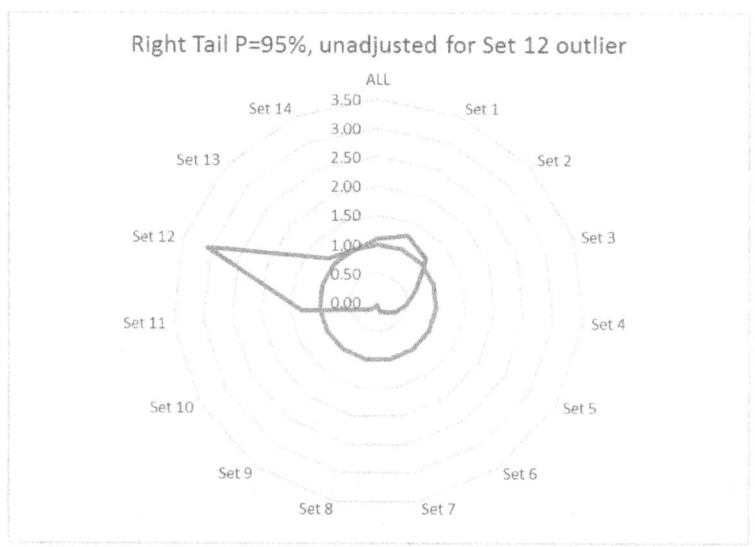

In the **center scenario** [P=0.50, $P(X<X_1)$ or $P(X>X_1)$], possible outliers were found in **Set 1** and **Set 2**. These sets correspond to the most recent two 10-year periods:

>**Set 1 (2016-2007):** RRCG was *near zero* (4.92E-04), SPG was .082 and the ratio of SPG/RRCG was 167.5. This compares to a ratio of 1.46 for the entire dataset (2016-1988).

>**Set 2 (2015-2006):** RRCG was .0135, SPG was .05383 and the ratio of SPG/RRCG was 3.99. This compares to a ratio of 1.46 for the entire dataset (2016-1988).

Adjusting for Outliers and Caveats. Adjustments are avoided wherever possible. Of the 75 computed ratio data points, the three outliers noted above were viewed as significant enough to warrant some form of adjustment to facilitate visual representation. **Method**. It was hoped that any adjustment could be made in a manner that would not excessively comprise representation of the data. The decision was made to use the fitted distribution for the "ALL" category (the entire dataset) rather than the fitted distribution for that *individual 10-year set*. This helped bring the ratios back into a similar range and generate a more readable chart.

However, it should be noted that the reasons for the outlier in certain periods should be examined more closely. For example, the center Set 1 scenario described above suggests an abnormal discrepancy between the fundamentals of essentially *no growth* and substantial stock price growth which should not be ignored. The fact that a similar pattern of "disconnect" was observed for Set 2 as well suggests possible manipulation to the upside in terms of stock price.

An attempt at identifying so-called regime changes over time periods is made later in this study.

Scenarios and Interpretation

The ratios for three scenarios corresponding to selected probabilities are shown below in radar charts:

Right Tail [P=0.95, P(X<X_1) or P=0.05, P(X>X_1)];

Left Tail [P=0.05, P(X<X_1)]; and

Center [P=0.50, P(X<X_1) or P(X>X_1)].

The circles within the radar charts are added to provide an easier visual comparison with the "perfect" alignment (ratio of 1.0) for all sets.

Right Tail Scenario [P=0.95, P(X<X_1) or P=0.05, P(X>X_1)]

This scenario may also be abbreviated as the "right tail P=0.95 scenario" or simply as P=95%.

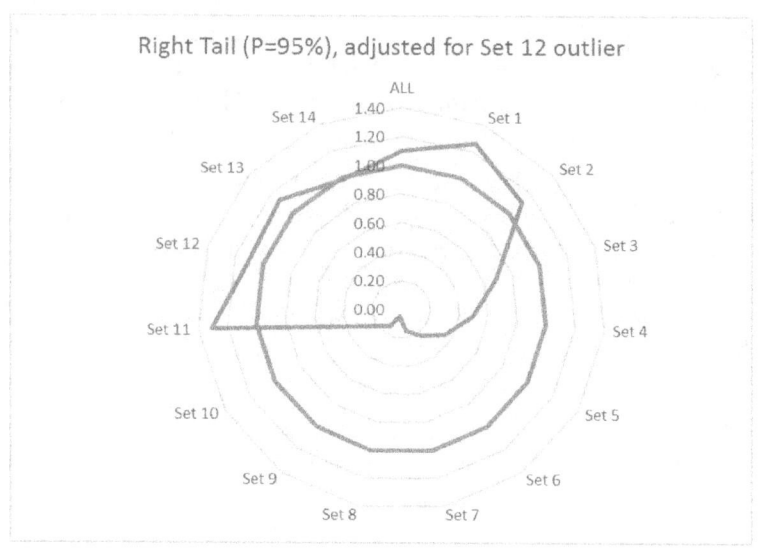

Right Tail (P=95%), adjusted for Set 12 outlier

Interpretation of results. In this right tail scenario, overvaluation is assumed to have occurred when the line falls outside of the circle: The "ALL" set, Set 1, Set 2, Set 11, Set 12, Set 13. Undervaluation is assumed to have occurred when the ratios appear inside the circle. Recall that this chart is adjusted for a single outlier in Set 12.

Left Tail Scenario [P=0.05, P(X<X₁)]

This scenario may also be abbreviated as the "left tail P=0.05 scenario" or as P=5%.

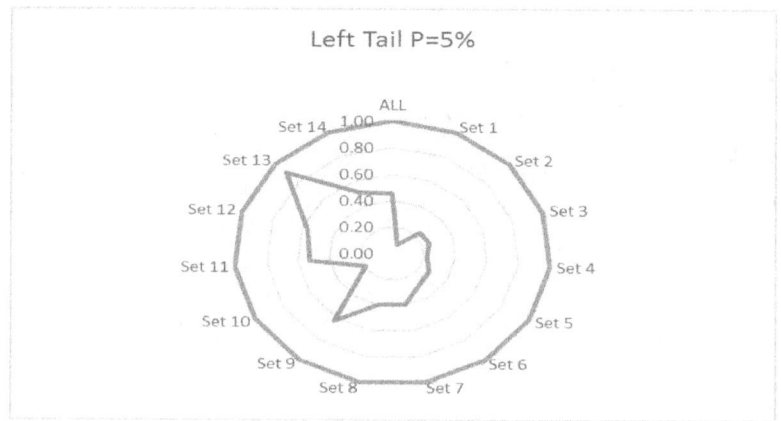

Left Tail P=5%

Interpretation of results. In the left tail at P=0.05, overvaluation is assumed to have occurred when the line remains inside of the circle. This appears to be quite consistent over the observation period (entire dataset and individual 10-year sets).

Center Scenario [P=0.50, P(X<X₁) or P(X>X₁)]

This scenario may also be abbreviated as the "center P=0.50 scenario" or as P=50%.

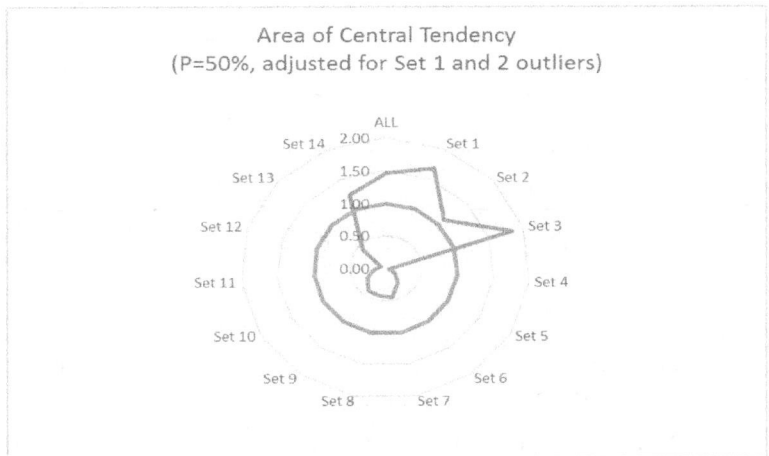

Area of Central Tendency
(P=50%, adjusted for Set 1 and 2 outliers)

Interpretation of results. In the central area, overvaluation is assumed to have occurred when the line is outside of the circle as seen in the "ALL" set, Set 1, Set 2. Set 3, and Set 14. Undervaluation is assumed to have occurred inside the circle. Recall that this chart is adjusted for outliers in Sets 1 and 2.

Summary of Valuation and Mispricing Results

The results are compiled here for all scenarios for all datasets including the one entire dataset (labelled "ALL") for 2016-1988. **Scenarios.** Although only 3 scenarios (left P=0.05, right P=0.95 and center P=.95) are shown above, in all there were a total of 5 scenarios (left P=0.05 and 0.10; right P=0.90 and P=0.95 and center P=0.50). **Datasets.** In total there were 15 datasets comprised of 14 10-year sets and the one entire dataset (i.e.

"ALL"). Therefore, the total number of ratios examined were 75 = 5 scenarios x 15 datasets. There were 5 ratios corresponding to the 5 scenarios for each *entire* dataset (i.e. "ALL"). Excluding those 5 ratios, there were 75-5=70 datasets of 10-year sets. Refer to the table below:

VALUATIONS (ALL SCENARIOS, ALL SETS)		Percentage of Total	
Category	# Ratios Computed	Overvaluation	Undervaluation
All Ratios for All Sets	75	61%	39%
10-yr Sets only	70	59%	41%
Entire Dataset (2016-1988)	5	100%	0%
Recent (3)*	15	87%	13%

*Note: **Recent (3)** refers to the most recent 3 10-year datasets

Interpretation of Results. As seen in the first two rows of the table above, there is a strong tendency towards overvaluation: This overvaluation proportion ranges between 59-61%.

In the third row which shows the results for the 5 scenarios for the entire dataset which spans 2016-1988, overvaluation occurs for *all* scenarios (100%) within the fitted probability distributions which were Gen. Extreme Value for RRCG and Johnson SB for the SPG.

As seen in the last row of the table marked "Recent (3)", the trend of overvaluation appears to be rising recently. "Recent (3)" refers to the *most recent* 3 10-year sets for all 5 scenarios which are Set 1 (2016-2007), Set 2 (2015-2006), and Set 3 (2014-2005).
Note: Recent (2) and Recent (1) are not shown in the table but *100% of the ratios* were found to be in the overvaluation range for each.
In conclusion, the results suggest a strong tendency towards overvaluation across the spectrum: On the upside (right tail), central area (center), and the downside (left tail), with a rising trend of overvaluation in recent years.

Divergence Viewed in Time Series

The following two charts compare SPG to RRCG for (a) changes in compound annual growth rates (abbreviated CAGR) and (b) Year-over-year changes (abbreviated YoY). The compound annual growth rate changes are presented as a "smoother" alternative and are computed using a 3-year moving average.

Over/undervaluation is evidenced by gap between the stock price variable SPG and the underlying fundamental variable (RRCG): Asset mispricing in terms of *overvaluation* is assumed to occur when the stock price change (SPG) exceeds the change in RRC (RRCG): *Overvaluation* is visually represented by black bars in the charts and white bars indicate *undervaluation* scenarios.

Interpretation. The period 1996 to 2000 suggests a general tendency towards overvaluation, followed by a reversal to undervaluation that began with a marked rise in 2001-2, followed by a declining trend through 2006. * Since 2007, the tendency appears to be towards overvaluation, to varying degrees.

It may be of interest to compare valuation turning points to significant events in financial history such as the NASDAQ bubble and crash in March 2000, 9-11, and the financial crisis of 2008 (followed by the stock market low of March 2009). It could be concluded that the market turmoil of 2000 and 2001 was reflected in the valuation (undervaluation). However, during and since the financial crisis of 2008 overvaluation tends to be the norm, with a tendency towards some recent alignment between the stock price growth (SPG) and fundamental variable RRCG. See the charts below:

68

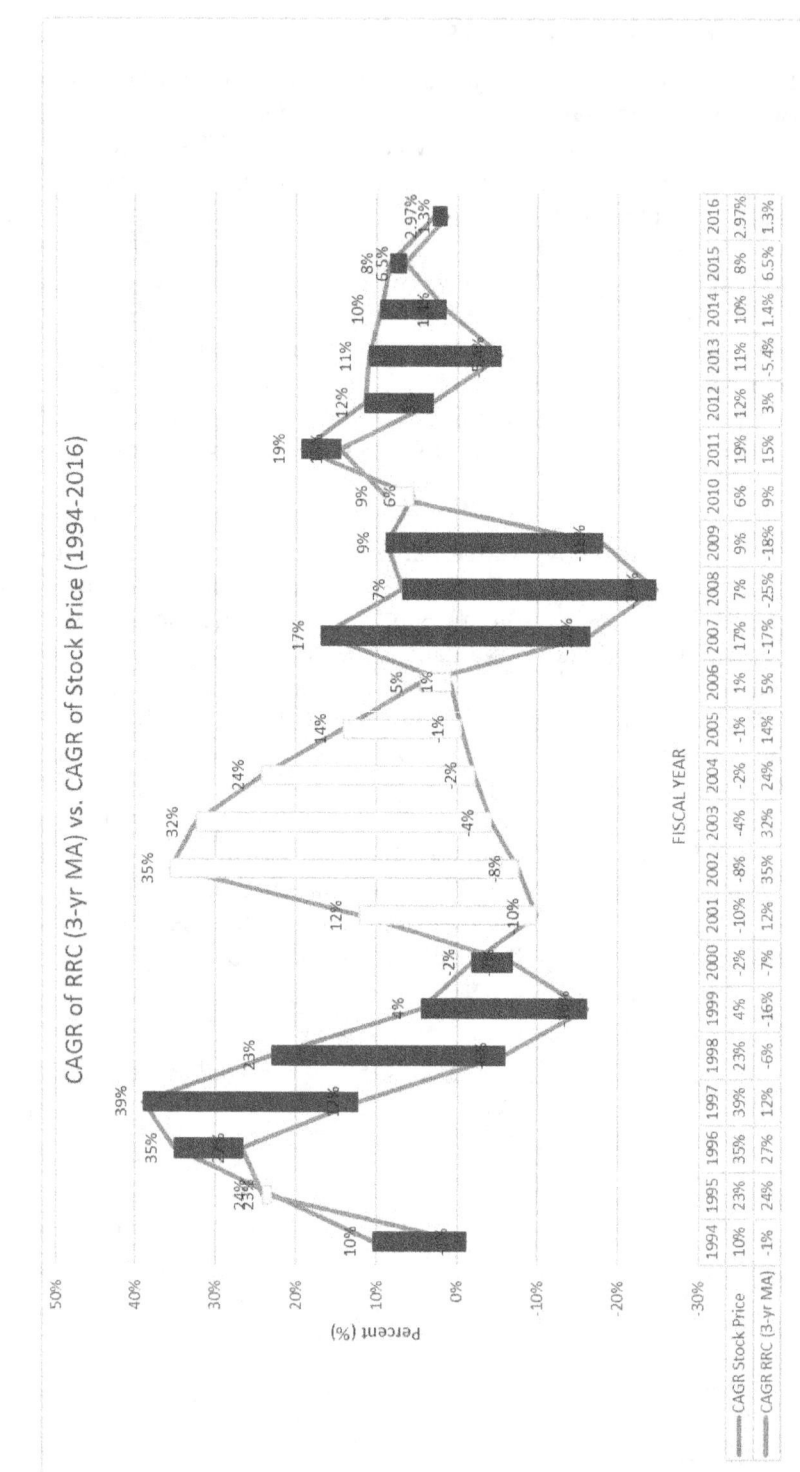

CAGR of RRC (3-yr MA) vs. CAGR of Stock Price (1994-2016)

FISCAL YEAR	1994	1995	1996	1997	1998	1999	2000	2001	2002	2003	2004	2005	2006	2007	2008	2009	2010	2011	2012	2013	2014	2015	2016
CAGR Stock Price	10%	23%	35%	39%	23%	4%	-2%	-10%	-8%	-4%	-2%	-1%	1%	17%	7%	9%	6%	19%	12%	11%	10%	8%	2.97%
CAGR RRC (3-yr MA)	-1%	24%	27%	12%	-6%	-16%	-7%	12%	35%	32%	24%	14%	5%	-17%	-25%	-18%	9%	15%	3%	-5.4%	1.4%	6.5%	1.3%

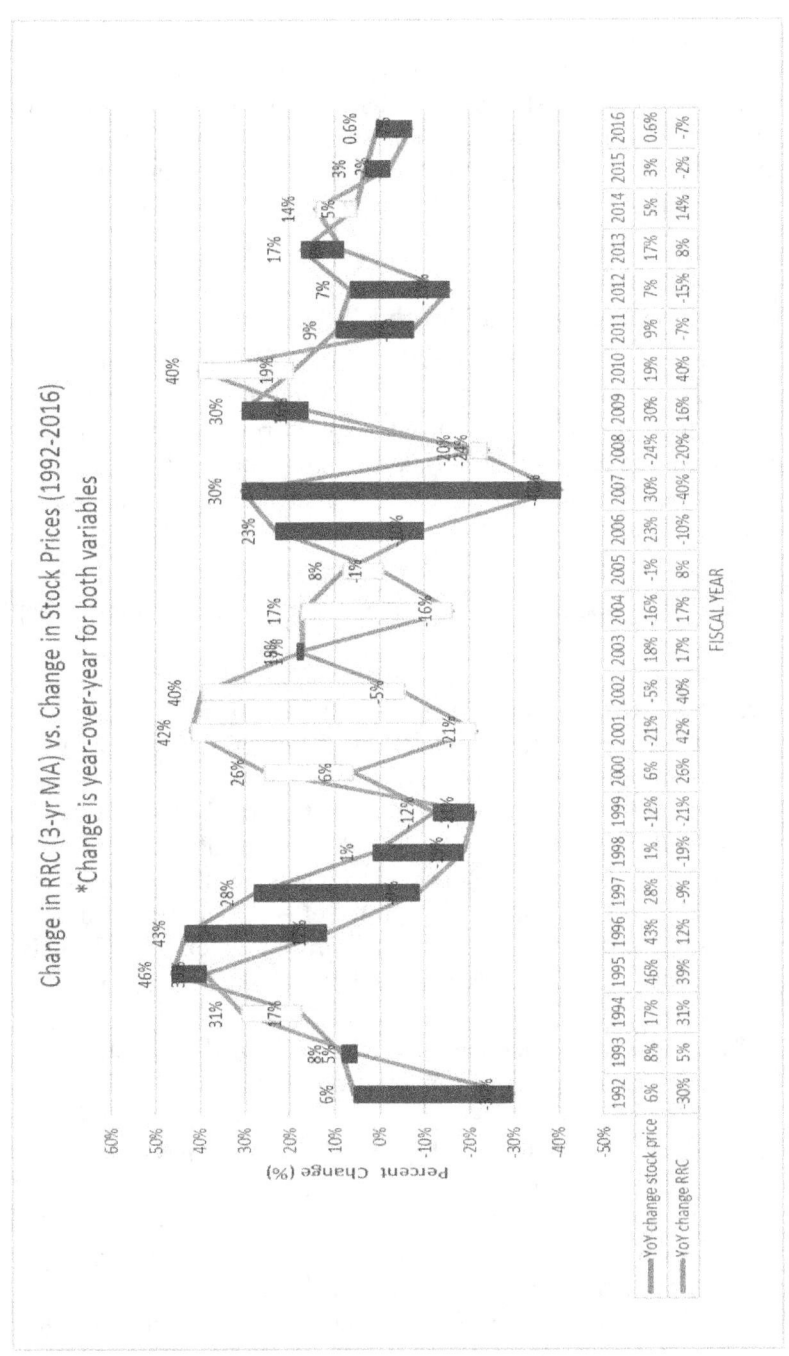

Change in RRC (3-yr MA) vs. Change in Stock Prices (1992-2016)
*Change is year-over-year for both variables

FISCAL YEAR	1992	1993	1994	1995	1996	1997	1998	1999	2000	2001	2002	2003	2004	2005	2006	2007	2008	2009	2010	2011	2012	2013	2014	2015	2016
YoY change stock price	6%	8%	17%	46%	43%	28%	1%	-12%	6%	-21%	-5%	18%	-16%	-1%	23%	30%	-24%	30%	19%	9%	7%	17%	5%	3%	0.6%
YoY change RRC	-30%	5%	31%	39%	12%	-9%	-19%	-21%	26%	42%	40%	17%	17%	8%	-10%	-40%	-20%	16%	40%	-7%	-15%	8%	14%	2%	-7%

In conclusion, both charts suggest a tendency towards overvaluation, with some evidence of alignment between the stock price growth SPG and fundamental variable RRCG. As of 2016, both charts suggest some overvaluation "gap," most strongly confirmed by the YoY chart with an overvaluation gap of 7.5 percentage points in 2016 compared to 1.7 percentage points for the CAGR chart.

Dual Decline Events: REVG and EI%

Declines in both *revenue growth* (REVG) and *equity income as a percentage of revenues* (EI%) in the *same* fiscal year may be a unique indicator of financial trouble for a firm. Therefore, if stock prices do not reflect these "dual declines" occurring in a given year, there might be a special case for evidence of asset mispricing and distortion.

Over the period 1988-2016, dual declines occurred *twice*, in 1998, and 2015, or about 7% of all observations. The details of each year are as follows:

In 2015, EI% declined to 12% from 17% the prior year while revenue growth was almost *negative* 4%.

In 1998, EI% declined to 6% from 9.8% the prior year while revenue growth was slightly below zero.

Between the two double decline events, clearly 2015 was the worst. Following the 2015 double decline, while there is some indication slowing of stock price growth as per the above charts, it is unclear whether this sufficiently reflected the seriousness of the event. Improved outlook for the firm's longer-term financial performance may have compensated for the dual decline in 2015.

Refer to Appendix 2 and Kennedy (2014) for additional details on fundamentals and the *equity income* variable.

C. Financial Distortion in Equity Financing: Recognition of Taxpayer Ownership.

Low-Cost Financing Source. A source of financial distortion that is often overlooked but that deserves mention concerns taxpayer funds that are transferred to firms in the form of either contracts or so-called *corporate welfare* including *subsidies* and *bailouts*.

This is a form of *low-cost financing* for businesses because the ownership rights of taxpayers are not recognized and there is no reimbursement to taxpayers for their infusion of capital into the companies. This issue was previously raised in Kennedy (2017), and the relevant policies discussed here are classified in the Subsystem 1 Policy Table as follows **Granting/Awarding of Contracts (Sub 1.2a)** and **Corporate Welfare (Sub1.4)**.

Note: Other redistributive policy actions such as **Transfer Payments (Sub1.1)** and **Employee Compensation: System 2 Employees (Sub1.3)**, are not considered here.

Recoupling

The concept of recoupling converts the flows of *income-based fees* (i.e. taxes) which are the *derivative inflows* to System 2 into *assets* with ownership rights preserved. In other words, the flow of funds is converted into a *stock* (an asset that preserves ownership rights), as shown in this circle and in the diagram further below:

Polarity Reversal This recoupling approach also reverses the polarity of the system such that the positive feedback loop structure is redirected and converted into a new type of *counterbalancing* feedback loop.

Flow-to-Asset Conversion Loop. Adding the recoupling link to the existing systems yields the following diagram:

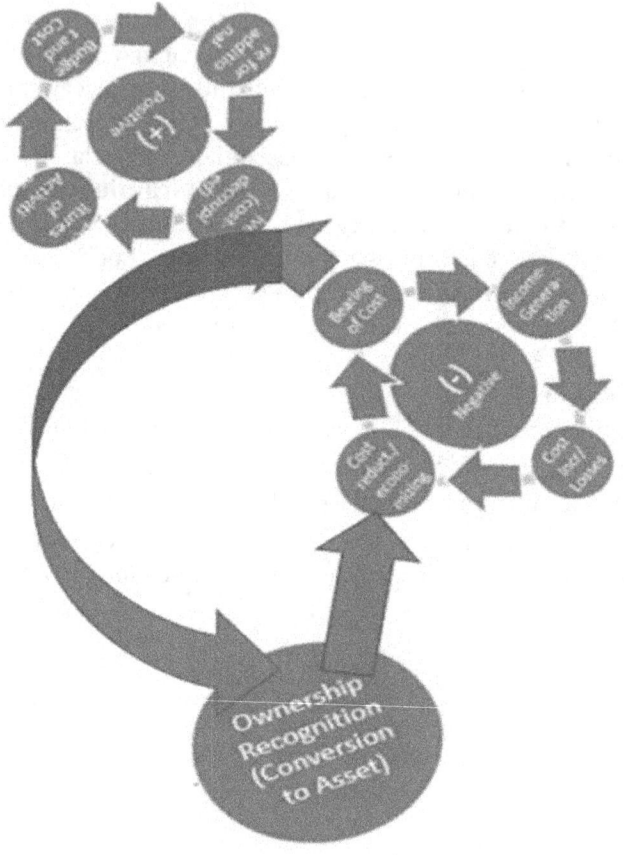

Source: Kennedy (2017) with flow-to-asset conversion loop added here.

Summary. Taxpayer funds are redistributed through the *granting/awarding of contracts* or *corporate welfare*. To recap from above, this benefits firms by giving them a much lower financing cost than would otherwise be the case. The recoupling approach proposed here rectifies this significant distortion of capital pricing for firms. Taxpayers retain legal ownership of their funds which are securitized and recorded as capital infusions to the firm. There might be the option to specify whether the funds are to be converted into (1) ownership/shares or (2) bonds/debt capital or (3) a mix of the two. The process might be governed under a form of legal trusteeship under which share ownership can be transferred to designated pension accounts or held directly by the taxpayers themselves in their own accounts. Taxpayers can receive a return on their "investment" in the form of dividends and or interest (along with principal repayment). The accounting methodology is detailed below.

Note that additional equity issuance will dilute the shares of the recipient firms (Re: *dilution*). It is acknowledged that any attempts to alter the existing arrangement would not likely to be implemented politically. However, at some point if taxpayer funds were integrated into *smart contracts*, the ownership of those funds and asset characteristics could be retained (Re: crypto-assets; See Appendix 2 for brief discussion).

Recoupling Accounting Methodology
Example: Contracts and Contract Revenues to Firms. A single example is shown here of a hypothetical government contract that represents revenues to a firm. First, the taxpayer ownership rights are recognized. Returns to the taxpayers (e.g. in the form of *dividends* or as *debt service* (i.e. interest + principal repayment) are paid to the taxpayers just as they would to other investors as a return on their investment. **Simultaneous Recognition**. Second, while recognizing taxpayer ownership, the firm recognizes the revenues *simultaneously*. How is this possible?

An unconventional set of accounting standards would be necessary although possibly unacceptable for GAAP; nevertheless, the following is a sketch of the accounting logic to preserve taxpayer ownership rights.

Journal Entries. Consider the *journal entries* (abbreviated JE) for Revenues when a government contract is legally granted to a firm (note that for simplicity, we use cash sales and a no *percentage of completion* contract):

74

Journal Entry 1. Recognition of Contract Revenues

Cash..................xx

Revenues...............xx

The following example assumes the issuance of common stock to the taxpayers to recognize their ownership while *simultaneously* recognizing the revenues earned from the contract:

Journal Entry 2. Common Stock Issuance

Here are journal entries for the *issuance of common* stock (ignoring par and excess-of-par value):

Cash..................xx

Common Stock.........xx

Modification. However, **JE2** must be modified such that the *debit* is no longer cash (since cash has already been recognized in **JE 1** above). Therefore, a new method and account category are proposed in the modified **Journal Entry 2** below, which is a *non-cash* transaction that replaces the cash in **JE2**.

Journal Entry 2 (Modified). Recognition of Taxpayer Ownership in Common Stock

Recognition of Ownership Rights................xx

Common Stock...............xx

The *recognition of ownership rights* account represents an *intangible asset* that recognizes the taxpayer ownership and serves as the offset to the common stock issued to them.

It is acknowledged that such a practice would significantly dilute the stock of the entity and businesses and would be opposed by existing investors.

Amortization. The account may be amortized according to a formula derived from estimated future *stock repurchases*.

***

APPENDICES

CONTENTS
A1. Distribution Fitting
A2. Fundamentals and Pricing
A3. Dynamic Empirical Probability Distributions
A4. Policy and System Dynamics Overview

APPENDIX 1. Distribution Fitting

Introduction and Shortcomings

It is commonly assumed that financial and economic variables conform to a normal (Gaussian) probability distribution. However, normality may not properly reflect the likelihood of real events and therefore may be an invalid assumption. This is particularly a concern in the financial realm where considerable interdependence may exist among key variables, some of which may exert an outsized force upon the others.

If the assumption of normality is not supported by empirical evidence, measures of the sample mean (average) may be an inappropriate and misleading indicator of the *true* mean. Even in scientific work: "...(S)cientists ...do not look for these (infinitely many different types of bell curves) and thus do not statistically test for this. ... thick-tailed bell curves get little or no attention." (Cook 2008).

Sample Size. It is recognized that sample sizes of the datasets were small due to the challenge of obtaining financial data of individual firms from their financial statements for extended observation periods. (Re: Law of Large Numbers)

An attempt to compensate for this shortcoming was to examine any regularities among the datasets, including a high relative frequency of certain fitted distributions or distribution types, to be detailed further below.

Error as Integral to Estimation. In Part III, caveats were provided in the notes to section on accounting for estimation error. Even given variables that behave in accordance with a normal Gaussian distribution, the critical problem of *explosive*

76

uncertainty remains due to minute imprecisions in parameter estimation itself. The uncertainty compounds with fat tails which are noted next.

Fat Tailed Distributions. The importance of *fat tails* (in which the ratio of the probabilities is much higher in the tails than in the body of the distribution) and the non-computability of tail events cannot be overemphasized, with serious implications for risk management. Moreover, it should not be assumed that fat tails are uncommon occurrences in economic life (Taleb 2012: 455; Also re: Cirillo, Fontanari and Taleb 2017; Cook 2008, 2017; Douady and Taleb 2012; Sandis and Taleb 2014; Taleb 2017).

Estimates of Probability. It should be emphasized that any estimates of probabilities are not intended to be predictive, nor should they be considered as having been "measured." At best, the results might be viewed as a "...speculative estimation of what *can* happen." (Taleb 2012: 462). (italics in original) Also re: concepts of *meta-uncertainty* and *meta-probability*.

Despite these and other shortcomings, by applying distribution-fitting techniques to the historical financial data it is hoped that we can learn more not only about some possible elementary properties and behavior of the variables of interest, but also to gain insights into the presence of asset mispricing/financial distortions examined in Part III applying the fitted distributions.

An alternative to distribution-fitting is to simply arrange the data into *relative frequency distributions* (rfds) for a rough visual representation of *empirical probabilities;* rfds can be referred to as empirical probability distributions (Spiegel, et al.2006). These rfds are shown in Appendix 3 for all five variables studied.

Distribution Fitting

Data. The data consists of financial data of a single non-financial firm in the consumer goods sector that operates in all geographic regions (worldwide). Financial data are sourced directly from the firm's audited financial statements as presented in the 10-K reports filed with the U.S. Securities and Exchange Commission. The firm's estimated market capitalization by then end of 2017 was approximately $U.S. 200 billion. The observations are annual, covering the fiscal years 1988 to 2016; since the company's fiscal year (FY) is on a calendar basis, the fiscal year corresponds to the calendar years (e.g. FY 2015 is the calendar year 2015).

Variables. Five variables were studied: Equity income as a percentage of revenues (abbreviated as EI or EI%), rate of return on cost (RRC), *changes* in RRC (RRCG), *changes* in stock price (SPG), *changes* in revenues (REVG). The "G" for variables of change refers to "growth" or "change" which can be positive/increasing, negative/decreasing or zero. Changes were annual (fiscal year and calendar year were the same). RRCG was computed as the compounded annual growth rate (CAGR) of the 3-yr moving average; a moving average was used to smooth the annual data which was fairly volatile. SPG was computed as the 3-year CAGR.

Datasets
Description of Datasets. The observations for each variable were divided into two types of datasets, each of which are detailed further below. (1) the entire sample for *each* variable (abbreviated as "ALL" in some charts); (2) 10-year subsamples (abbreviated as "10-year sets" or "sets"). It should be clarified that 10-year sets were designed to match the amortization of the hypothetical 10-year term loan to compute or estimate the interest rates (CBI and CNRI) for such a loan; (recall that the 10-year term loan has a *matching* term and amortization, abbreviated as "10/10").

1. Entire Sample of Each Variable: 5 Datasets. This is abbreviated as the "ALL" category: Note that this abbreviation "all" refers to the entire sample of a *particular* variable. Because there were five key variables, there were a total of five such datasets. Details are shown for each variable in order, here:
Variable; # Observations; Fiscal years
EI: 29, 1988-2016
RRC: 29, 1988-2016
RRCG: 26, 1991-2016
SPG: 27, 1990-2016

REVG: 33, 1984-2016
Total: 5 datasets (5 variables x entire sample of each variable).

2. 10-Year Subsamples: 99 Datasets (10-year periods, sequential, shifted by one year). The subsamples each cover ten-year periods, and may be abbreviated "10-year sets" or "sets." These sets were created by shifting each 10-year period by one year each. For example, "Set 1" was the most recent, covering the 10-year period 2016-2007 (the most recent year appears first), "Set 2" was 2015-2006, and so on until a 10-year period was no longer possible due to lack of previous historical data. In total, there were 99 sets of these 10-year subsamples for all 5 variables combined. Details for each variable are provided here:

Variable; # Sets; Fiscal Years (starting, ending)
EI: 20, 1988-2016
RRC: 20,1988-2016
RRCG: 17, 1991-2016
SPG: 18, 1990-2016
REVG: 24, 1984-2016
Total 10-Year Sets: 99

In total, there were 104 datasets, consisting of the 5 datasets of the "ALL" category, and the 99 datasets of the 10-year subsamples.

Goodness-of-Fit Testing. Goodness-of-fit tests are used to test if a sample of the data comes from a population with a specific distribution. Three different tests are used here: The Kolmogorov-Smirnoff, Anderson-Darling and Chi-Squared tests (which may be abbreviated K-S, A-D, and Chi, respectively). The Kolmogorov-Smirnoff test (Kolmogorov 1933; Smirnoff 1948; Chakravarti 1967) is initially used as the "default" for the best fit as determined by the K-S test statistic with the highest rank (#1). However, the K-S rank is also compared to that of the Anderson-Darling test (Anderson and Darling 1952; Stephens 1974, 1986) and Chi-Squared test (Snecedor and Cochran 1989) to determine whether another distribution might be more justified. "Several goodness-of-fit tests, such as the Anderson-Darling test and the Cramer-Von Mises test, are refinements of the K-S test. As these refined tests are generally considered to be more powerful* than the original K-S test, many analysts prefer them" (NIST 2012: 1.3.5.16). The Chi-Squared test can be applied to discrete distributions unlike the K-S and A-D tests which are limited to continuous distributions, but the Chi-Squared statistic is not valid without a sufficiently large sample size.

*Notes: "Powerful" is in the sense that the particular test detects a difference when a difference does in fact exist. For the computations, the maximum number of iterations of MLE (maximum likelihood estimates) were limited to 100.

Results of Goodness-of-Fit Testing

1. Entire Sample of Each Variable: 5 Datasets. Recall that these variables are: Equity income as a percentage of revenues (EI%), RRC, changes in RRC (RRCG), changes in stock price (SPG), and changes in revenues (REVG). The best-fitting distribution as determined by *goodness of fit* testing, is shown below, along with the parameters of the fitted distribution. To clarify, a best fit does not necessarily mean that the "correct" or "true" distribution was found (also re: *meta-uncertainty*; *meta-probability*)

The top-ranked distribution (#1) according to the K-S test is reported in bold-face type, followed by its estimated parameters and the K-S statistic. **Comparing Test Results.** Next, the A-D rank was compared with the K-S rank. If the A-D rank was either #1 or #2 for the *same* distribution as the K-S, then that distribution was deemed as reasonably the best fit. However, if the top-ranked distribution based on the A-D test differed from that of the K-S test and *both* the K-S and A-D ranks were either #1 or #2, that alternative distribution is noted, along with its rank# according to both tests and the A-D statistic. A high A-D rank# *combined with a high K-S rank#* is viewed as stronger support for the best fit, and an asterisk is placed next to the fitted distribution with this determination; the corresponding overall highest ranked distribution. *Note that the charts of the fitted distributions may be somewhat compressed due to page space considerations.*

1. Equity income (EI%)
Dagum (4P) (0.20966; 10.529; 0.20942; 0.0281)
K-S Statistic: 0.05683. (A-D Rank: #5)
***Johnson SB** (K-S rank #2, A-D rank #1); A-D Statistic: 0.1161.

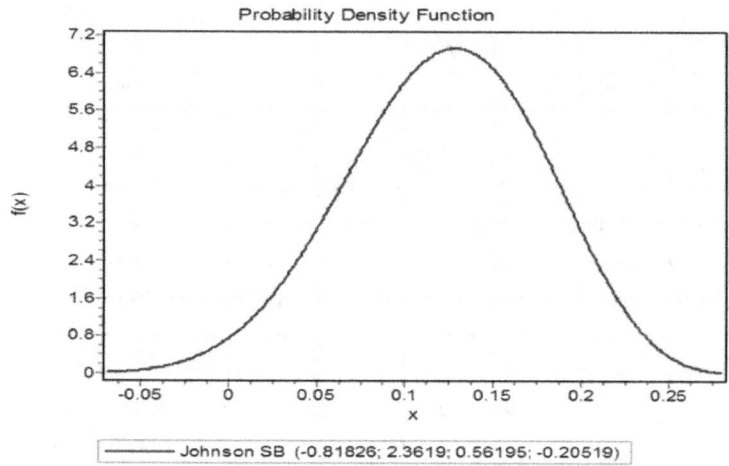

2. Rate of Return on Cost (RRC)
Dagum (4P) (0.23545; 7.872; 0.238; 0.02148)
K-S Statistic: 0.05576. (A-D rank: #11)
***Johnson SB** (K-S Rank #2, A-D Rank #1); A-D Statistic: 0.11751.

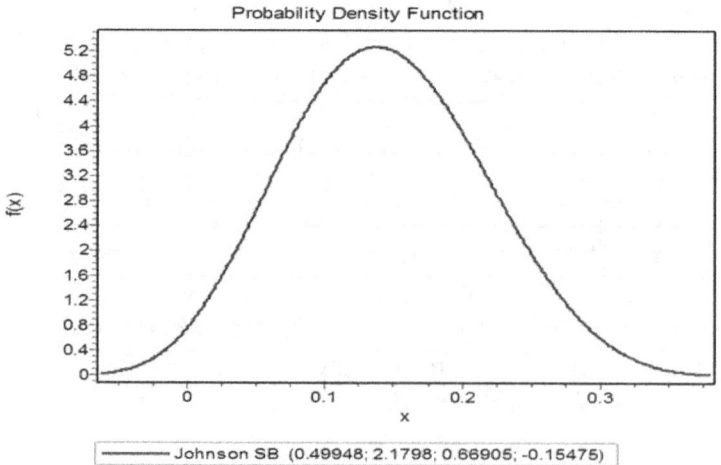

3. Changes in Rate of Return on Cost (RRCG)
Gen. Extreme Value (0.22606; 0.16346; -0.00836)
K-S Statistic: 0.06447. (A-D Rank: #2).
Anderson-Darling: Rank #2 (A-D Statistic: 0.142).

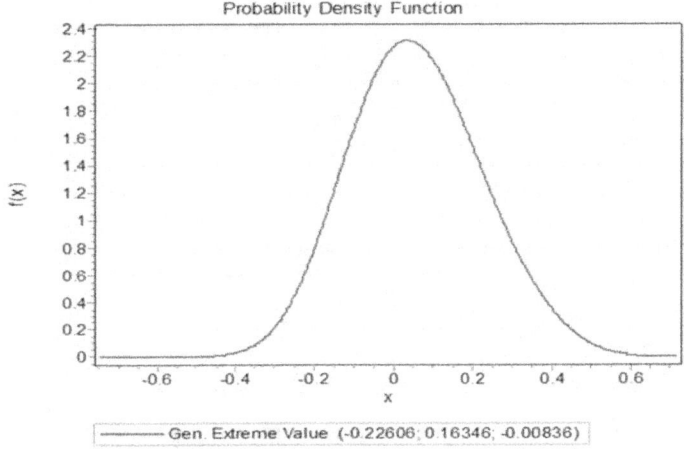

4. Changes in Stock Price (SPG)
Johnson SB (0.84538; 0.94002; 0.75005; -0.1452)
K-S and A-D rank #1 (K-S Statistic:0.05784; A-D Statistic:0.10467).

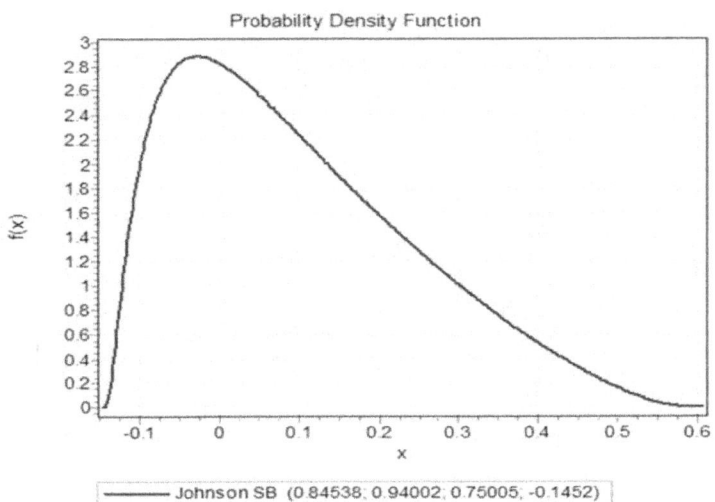

5. Changes in Revenues (REVG)
Wakeby (0.99517; 6.972; 0.07034; -0.01197; -0.1248)
K-S Statistic:0.05136. (A-D rank #16)
*Log-Logistic (3P) was ranked #2 for both the K-S and the A-D tests
(K-S Statistic:0.05521; A-D Statistic: 0.11575).

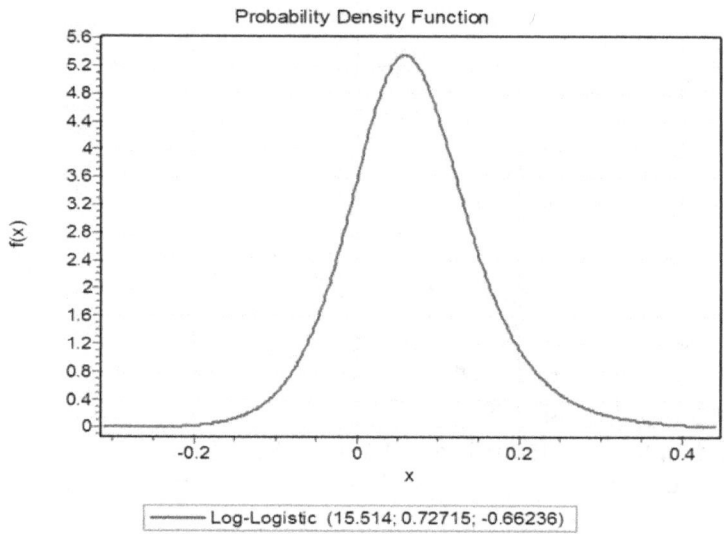

Although the Wakeby rank per the A-D test was considerably
lower, the fitted distribution is shown here for reference.

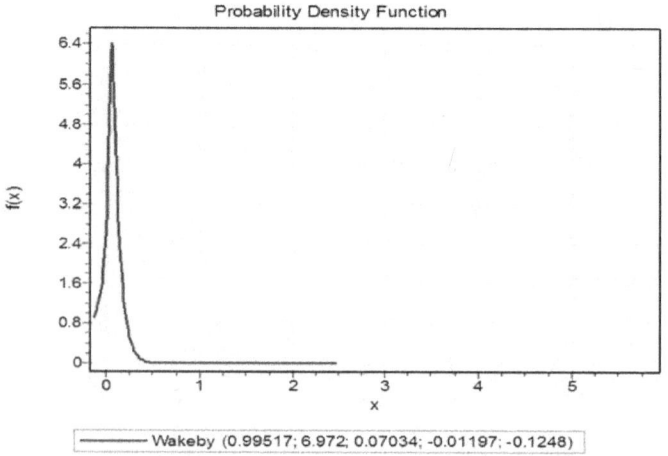

Normality. Lower-ranking fits were also examined to see if any fitted distributions were found to conform to a *normal* distribution; the only cases were as follows:

1. **RRCG** (#2 with the K-S test, and #5 with the A-D test)
2. **REVG** (#3 with the Chi-Squared test only).

Quantile-quantile plots (Q-Q plots) are not shown. However, the K-S goodness of fit test might be viewed as a reasonable quantification of the visual representation of a Q-Q plot. (Cook, 2017)

2. All Datasets (104)

The results for all 104 datasets are shown below, first as relative frequencies, and in radar charts. These fitted distributions are all based only on the top rank of the K-S test. It is recognized that consideration of the A-D or other tests might have yielded different results.

Relative Frequency. The top 10 most commonly occurring fitted distributions of the 104 sets are shown in the chart below in relative* frequencies.

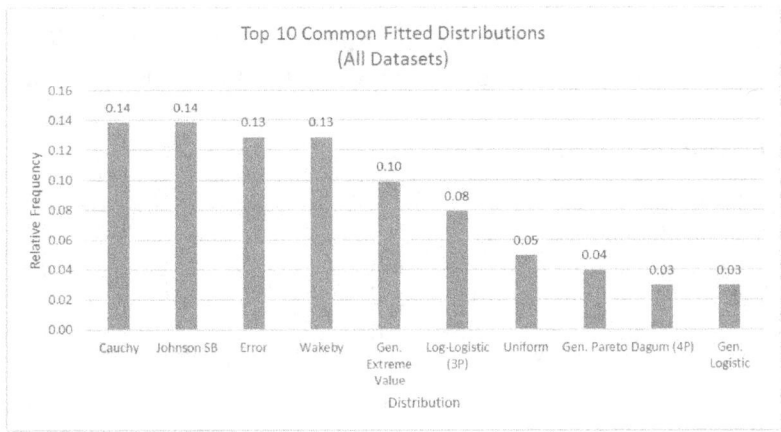

*The y-axis represents the relative frequency of the total (i.e. 0.10 is 10% of the total observations).

84

Distribution Types of All Datasets. The fitted distributions were also categorized primarily into 4 main continuous distribution types: Bounded, unbounded, non-negative and advanced. The range of bounded ("B") distributions is points "a" and "b." The range of unbounded ("U") distributions is -∞ to +∞. The advanced distributions do not fit into the "B" "U" or non-negative (NN) categories. The relative frequency of occurrence is shown in the chart below:

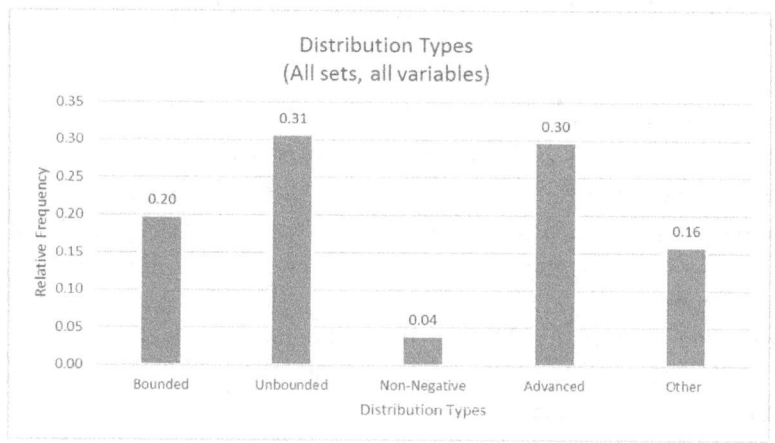

The following relates the distribution type to the fitted distributions with relative frequency (RelF) of 10% or more in the chart above:

Distribution	RelF	Type
Cauchy	0.14	Unbounded
Johnson SB	0.14	Bounded
Error	0.13	Unbounded
Wakeby	0.13	Advanced
Gen. Ex. Value	0.10	Advanced

All Datasets in Radar Charts. Radar charts are shown for each dataset for each variable *based solely on the K-S test* top ranking. At top of the chart (the 12 o'clock position) is "ALL" (the dataset of the entire sample for the particular variable). The individual 10-year datasets abbreviated "sets" are read clockwise from most recent, beginning with Set 1, Set 2 and so on clockwise to the earliest period. Recall that each set is a sequential 10-year period shifted by one year: Set 1 corresponds to the years 2016-2007, Set 2, 2015-2006, and so on. Numeric identifiers were assigned to the distributions due to chart space constraints.

Below the charts are listed the most frequently occurring distributions based on the K-S test, indicating the distribution name ("Name"), relative frequency ("RelF") and corresponding identifiers, respectively.

Uniformity of Distributions Case. If all the distributions were identical, there would be a perfect circular formation inside the radar chart. However, since the fitted distributions of the sets tend to differ, a star-like formation is most common.

1. Equity Income (EI%): 10-Year Sets + Entire Sample (ALL)

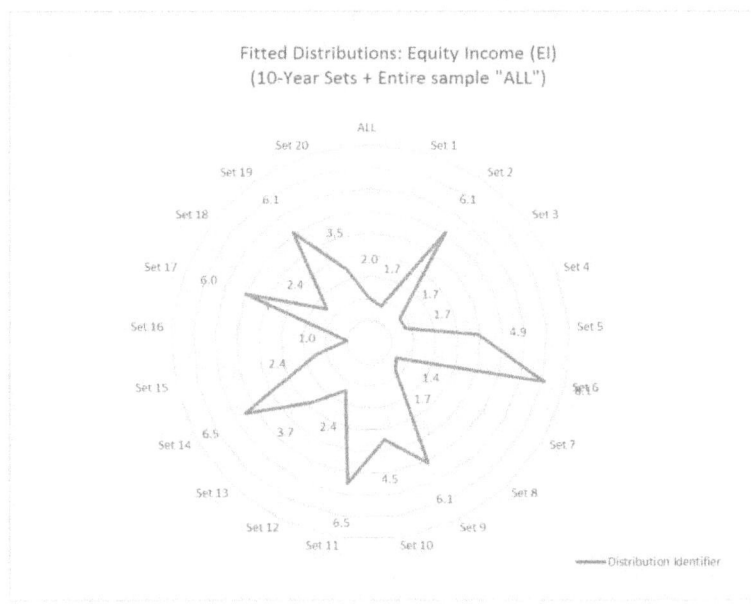

The fitted distributions, their relative frequency and identifier as shown in the chart are, respectively:

86

Name	RelF	Identifier
Cauchy	0.19	1.7
Error	0.14	2.5
Wakeby	0.14	6.1
Dagum	0.10	2.0

Dagum is 3P; RelF refers to relative frequency.

Recall from above that the Johnson SB distribution, though not appearing in high frequency for the 10-year sets, was found to be the highest ranked fit for the "ALL" observations (entire sample) category for both the K-S or A-D tests (K-S rank #2, A-D rank #1; A-D Statistic: 0.1161).

2. RRC: 10-Year Sets + Entire Sample (ALL)

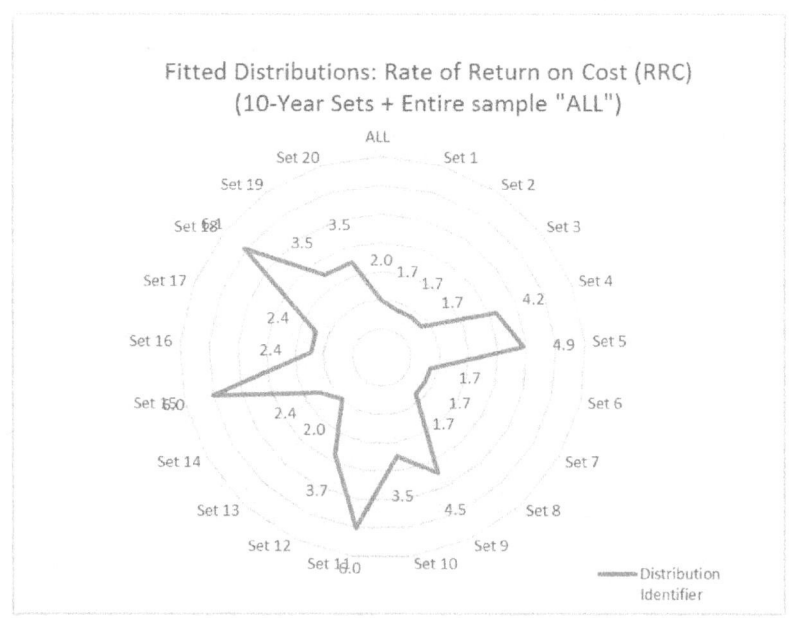

Name	RelF	Identifier
Cauchy	0.29	1.7
Error	0.14	2.4
GEV	0.14	3.5

GEV is Generalized Extreme Value; RelF refers to relative frequency.

Recall from above that the Johnson SB distribution, though not appearing in high frequency for the 10-year sets, was found to be the highest ranked fit for the entire sample (ALL) based on both the K-S and A-D tests (K-S rank #2, A-D rank #1; A-D Statistic: 0.11751).

3. RRCG: 10-Year Sets + Entire Sample (ALL)

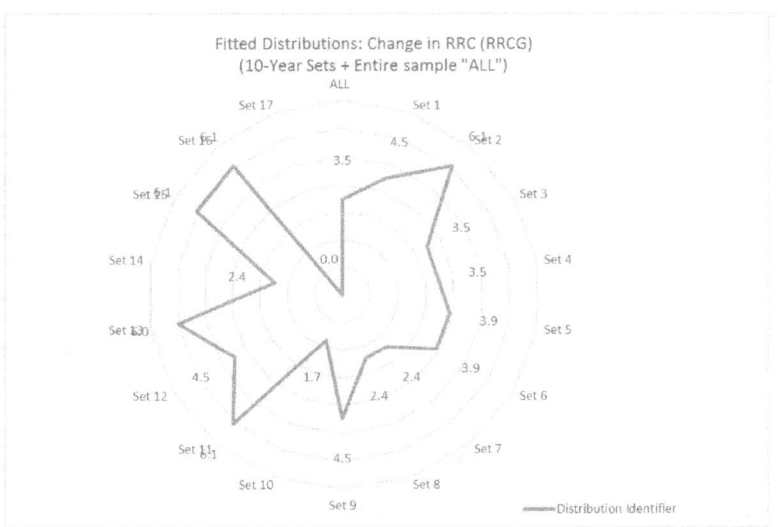

Name	RelF	Identifier
Wakeby	0.24	6.1
Error	0.18	2.4
Gen. Extreme Value*	0.18	3.5
Johnson SB	0.18	4.5

RelF refers to relative frequency.

*Recall from above that the Gen. Extreme Value distribution was also found to be the best fit for the entire sample (ALL) category based on both the K-S and A-D tests (K-S rank #1, A-D rank #2).

4. SPG: 10-Year Sets + Entire Sample (ALL)

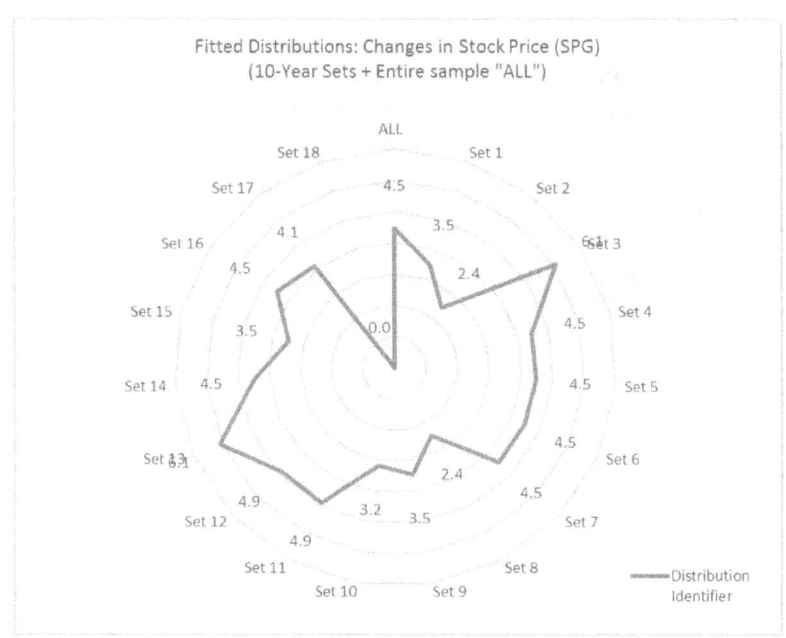

Name	RelF	Identifier
Error	0.10	2.4
Johnson SB*	0.35	4.5
Wakeby	0.15	6.1
Gen. Extreme Value	0.15	3.5

*Recall from above that for the entire sample (ALL), both the K-S and A-D tests ranked the Johnson SB distribution as #1.

5. REVG: 10-Year Sets + Entire Sample (ALL)

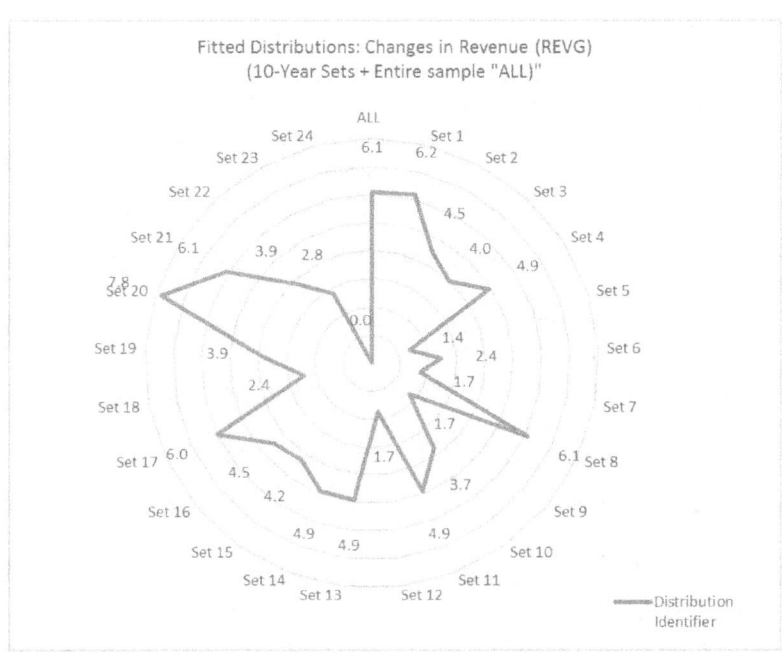

Name	RelF	Identifier
Log-Logistic (3P) *	0.17	4.9
Wakeby	0.13	6.1
Cauchy	0.13	1.7

*Recall from above that the Log-Logistic (3P) distribution, was ranked #2 for the entire sample (ALL) based on both the K-S and A-D tests (K-S Statistic: .05521; A-D Statistic: .11575).

Regime Changes Among 10-Year Sets

Regime changes are said to occur when there is some type of disruption in the observed pattern of fitted distributions for the sets. A "regime" itself was defined simply as a *run* (repeat) of the same distribution for 3 or more years. It should be emphasized that this is an exceedingly cursory analysis.

Note that the best-fitting distribution results are based solely on the K-S test: It is thus possible that the top-ranked distributions based on other goodness-of-fit tests (e.g. A-D, Chi) might have produced different results, but this was not examined due to time limitations.

The sample examined was from 1997 to 2016 consisting of the 10-year sets of the five variables: EI and RRC (20 sets each), RRCG (17 sets), SPG (18 sets), and REVG (24 sets). Regimes identified according to the simple criterion above were as follows (the variable, sets of the repeating distributions and corresponding years are indicated):

RRC (2 runs of 3 years each, Cauchy for both runs):
Set 1 (2016-2007), Set 2 (2015-2006), Set 3 (2014-2005)
Set 6 (2011-2002), Set 7 (2010-2001), Set 8 (2009-2000).
SPG (1 run of 4 years, Johnson SB)
Set 4 (2013-2004), Set 5 (2012-2003), Set 6 (2011-2002),
Set 7 (2010-2001)

Uniformity: Entire Sample and Subsamples
Also of interest was how often the fitted distribution for the entire sample of each variable (ALL) matched the individual 10-year sets for the same variable.

Recall that for the entire sample, some comparisons were made between the K-S and A-D tests to determine a possibly better "alternative" fit. The fitted distributions for the 10-year sets were based solely on the K-S test.

Initial Best Fit. From above, the best fitted distribution for the entire sample of each variable is shown here *based on the K-S test alone*, followed by the relative frequency of 10-year sets (the percentage of the total) that *matched* the fitted distribution for the entire sample.

Variable	Distribution	Rel Freq	No# Sets
1 EI	Dagum(4P)	0%	20
2 RRC	Dagum(4P)	5%	20
3 RRCG	Gen. Extreme Val	12%	17
4 SPG	Johnson SB	33%	18
5 RevG	Wakeby	8%	24
Totals		**58%**	**99**

Note: Rel Freq total <100% is due to absence of matching distributions.

Alternative Best Fit. Taking into account *both* the K-S and A-D test results as discussed above, the *alternative* best fits are listed in the table below. The relative frequency of 10-year sets (the percentage of the total) that *matched* the fitted distribution for the entire sample are shown:

Variable	Distribution	Rel Freq	No# Sets
1 EI	Johnson SB	5%	20
2 RRC	Johnson SB	5%	20
3 RRCG	Gen. Extreme Val	12%	17
4 SPG	Johnson SB	33%	18
5 RevG	Log-Logistic	17%	24
Totals		**72%**	**99**

Note: Rel Freq total <100% is due to absence of matching distributions.

Tentative Results

The fitted distributions should not necessarily be viewed as "correct" or definitive; at best they might be viewed as estimates or approximations (see the *caveats* noted previously in the shortcomings of this Appendix as well as in Part III). The summary results for fitted distributions of the 10-year sets and the entire samples are treated separately below.

10-Year Sets

The fitted distributions of the 10-year sets varied considerably. However, the Cauchy distribution* had a strong presence in the variables EI and RRC at 19%, 29% of the total fitted distributions, respectively. The Wakeby was dominant for the RRCG variable with 24% of the total fitted distributions. The Johnson SB was the most frequently occurring for SPG at 35% of the total (which was also the highest relative frequency found for *any* variable). The Log-Logistic was fitted the most frequently at 17% of the total. Recall that the 10-year sets were fitted solely with the K-S test and results may have differed had comparisons been made with the other goodness-of-fit tests.

*Note: A special mention is made of the Cauchy distribution because of its frequent appearance among the fitted distributions. The Cauchy is also an example of a *ratio distribution* consisting of two independent, normal distributions. "The random variable associated with this distribution comes about as the ratio of two Gaussian (normal) distributed variables with zero mean." (*Wikipedia, "Ratio Distribution"*)

EI and RRC, 10-Year Sets: Among the fitted distributions of the 10-year sets, the Johnson SB appeared more frequently for the variable EI (5% of total) versus the Dagum (4P) (0% of total). For RRC, the Johnson SB and Dagum (4P) were equally represented (5% of total for each). Therefore, the Johnson SB is favored for EI, and not excluded from consideration as a reasonable representative distribution for RRC.

REVG, 10-Year Sets: The Log-Logistic distribution also appears more frequently among the 10-year sets (17% of the total for the Log-Logistic vs. 8% for the Wakeby).

Entire Sample

As for which distributions might be favored to the entire sample (ALL) of each variable any conclusions drawn should be thought of as tentative at best, and may not apply to any other related samples for the same variables--whether *subsamples* (such as the 10-year sets) of the entire sample, or the entire sample with *new* (future or past) observations added on.

RRCG, SPG: For the change variables RRCG and SPG, the Generalized Extreme Value and Johnson SB were chosen as the best representations of the entire samples, respectively, because not only were they the top ranked according to the K-S and A-D tests, but they also were prominently featured among the 10-year subsamples (18% and 35% of the total, respectively).

EI and RRC: As for the non-change variables EI and RRC, the Dagum (4P) was the best fit per the K-S test alone, but when considering both the A-D and the K-S test results together, the Johnson SB ranked highest.

REVG, Entire Sample: As noted previously, tor REVG the Wakeby ranked the highest per the K-S test, but which fell to a ranking of #16 by the A-D test. In contrast, the Log-Logistic was highly ranked by *both* the K-S and the A-D tests (#2 for each).

Functions, Parameters, and Domains. The probability density functions (pdfs)* of the tentative fitted distributions for each variable's entire sample are shown below.

Notes: 1. The Cauchy distribution, which appeared frequently among top-ranking fitted distributions for the 10-year sets per the K-S test, as well as individual parameters (continuous shape, scale, and location) and domain/support, are not shown. 2. The Wakeby is defined by a quantile function rather than by a pdf; it is not shown because as discussed above the Log-Logistic was higher ranked by both goodness-of-fit tests.

Johnson SB

$$f(x) = \frac{\delta}{\lambda \sqrt{2\pi} z(1-z)} \exp\left(-\frac{1}{2}\left(\gamma + \delta \ln\left(\frac{z}{1-z}\right)\right)^2\right)$$

where $z \equiv \dfrac{x - \xi}{\lambda}$

Generalized Extreme Value

$$f(s; \sigma, \xi) = \frac{1}{\sigma} \begin{cases} (1 + \xi s)^{(-1/\xi)-1} \exp(-(1+\xi s)^{-1/\xi}) & \xi \neq 0 \\ \exp(-s)\exp(-\exp(-s)) & \xi = 0 \end{cases}$$

Log-Logistic

$$f(x; \alpha, \beta) = \frac{(\beta/\alpha)(x/\alpha)^{\beta-1}}{(1 + (x/\alpha)^{\beta})^2}$$

Source: *Wikipedia*

APPENDIX 2. Fundamentals and Pricing

The idea behind fundamentals is that there is (are) some assumed source(s) of value upon which "true" value of an asset should be based, and the *price* of that asset should reflect this *true value* (although they may diverge considerably). Fundamentals might also be referred to as "drivers" of value.

When expressing the fundamentals relationship, the "price" variable is typically in the numerator and the chosen fundamental variable is in the denominator. The discussion below aims to provide a brief overview of fundamentals, including the related topics of prices and valuation.

Price, Value, and Pricing/Valuation. A distinction should be made between "price" and "value;" the topic can be confusing. To begin, the "price" is probably best clarified as what something can be bought and sold for *now* as determined by (an) actual, verifiable transaction(s). The concept of "price" is *dynamic* because prices for many things tend to fluctuate almost constantly. For some items (e.g. real estate) the price *now* may not be known yet so practically the "price" is referred to as the *most recent* price at which the asset was *sold* (Note that the *quantity* sold *at that price* may often be ignored but can be highly relevant; see the brief comments on *quantity* and *volume* below).

When describing the "price" not of an item, but of an *overall market*, the term *market capitalization* is often used (e.g. prices x number of shares, abbreviated "market cap.") In the stock market, for example, since the individual prices are being determined through numerous trades in real time market cap may be a reasonable estimate of the overall market's current "price."

When talking about the future, unless the item's price has been pre-determined by a *binding contractual sale*, it is clearer to say the *projected* (or hoped-for) price since the price for the item now may differ substantially from what it can be sold for in a month.

Also, "price" may differ from the *appraised value* (as in a real estate appraisal) since the property being appraised has not sold yet and therefore the actual selling price has not yet been determined. The appraisal is an estimate of what the appraiser thinks the property's price should be (typically based on comparable sales in the area).

The concept of *subjective value** is essential: People impute different values to the same thing based on their own personal reasons. Consider two people looking at a "fixer-upper" home. One sees a "dump" with no value and the other immediately puts a bid on the property for $200,000 because after paying the costs of repair and remodeling, they estimate that the house can be sold to cover the cost with a significant profit (surplus). As seen in this example, each person assigned a different value to (i.e. "priced") the asset: One priced it as zero (not buying), the other at $200,000.

*Re: *Subjective value theory*; Carl Menger, William Stanley Jevons, Leon Walras. On concepts in price theory and value, see De La Calle (1544) Re: School of Salamanca; Friedman (1986); Hayek (1931); Hicks (1946); Stigler (1987).

Worthlessness and Value. If subjective values are unanimous such that there is complete lack of demand for an item, there may be *no* market (no buyers or sellers); in this case *no price* exists and therefore the value of the item therefore can be assumed to be zero--worthless. However, this can change due to innovation: There is always the possibility that someone can take the item and potentially create value by re-purposing it into something new that sells, and a market for the item is born seemingly out of nowhere. This relates to the topic of *entrepreneurship* and *economic growth*.

Mispricing and Valuation. An item (asset) is deemed *mispriced* or over or under-valued if it does not reflect some theorized measure of its "true" value. This true value is based on the concept that there may be (one or more) fundamental sources of value, although it should be emphasized that there is unlikely to ever be a universal viewpoint on this difficult topic: In addition to fundamental analysis, there are many other analytical tools such as *technical* and *quantitative analysis.*

In financial language, the term *valuation* is used to describe a relationship between the price and fundamentals; when pointing out possible mispricing one might say that "stocks are trading at very high/low valuations."

Notes: 1. The pricing of *capital* relates to *interest rates* which omitted from this appendix because distortions and capital mispricing involving interest rates are covered in the main text of this book. An important consensus among economists of diverse views concerns *capital formation* (e.g. capital as equipment, machinery, and tools) as playing an essential role in economic growth and rising living standards (Marx 1867; Weil 2008). *Mispricing* of capital can lead to resource misallocation and economic dislocation; see Part I for historical references.

2. The term "value" also has an unrelated meaning which is to indicate *data points* (e.g. positive or negative *values*).

Quantity. It should also be emphasized that prices are inextricably associated with *quantities* of the item being sold: Even for the "same" unit price of $1 per unit of milk, substantially different *information* is being conveyed when comparing the following two different transactions: A single bulk sale of *100 units of milk* at $1/unit, and a sale of only *1 unit of milk* for $1/unit. The price per unit is the same, but one of the transactions can be considered *relatively* more expensive based on *quantity* sold at that price.

Another example is relevant to the recent rise of cryptocurrencies: When units can be divided into infinitesimally smaller portions, slivers of the currency can be sold such that the *unit* price can become astronomical. Consider 1 unit of bitcoin (1 BTC) with a 2017 market price of $10,000 per unit (i.e. 1 BTC=$10,000). Few can afford to buy a single coin for $10,000, but smaller and smaller quantities can be sold at higher *per unit* prices while remaining affordable: At $10,000 per unit, 0.0001 of a BTC is just $1. Now consider this same 0.0001 of a BTC being sold for $10: While the price has increased by 10 times, *at that quantity* it still may be reasonably affordable to many buyers. When those small quantities sold are summed at those prices, 1 unit of BTC is now being "valued" at $100,000. Another 10-fold increase from $10 to $100 for 0.0001 BTC means $1,000,000 *per unit* of BTC. However, does this mean that the "price" of a single unit is $1 million? Did any single buyer actually spend $1 million for a single unit? See below for further discussion on possible fundamentals in the crypto space as well as warnings.

In sum, *quantities* of items being sold should also be considered along with prices of the item being sold.

Related to the crucial concept of market *liquidity* are the trading *volume* and nature of market participation. Consider a simple example of an asset being traded at the *same price*, 100 shares of a stock traded: (a) thousands of times among hundreds of thousands of independent participants* in a day; (b) thousands of times among 50 participants in a day, 20 of whom have close affiliations with, and may often trade amongst, one another; (c) *once* in a day in either of scenarios (a) and (b). Even though the price per share is the same in all three "markets," how reliable are the prices? *

Also note that prices can fluctuate wildly depending on market conditions. Ideally there is some balance between buyers and sellers in a market so that their buy-sell orders can be matched up; market-makers earn a spread for handling the trades with little or no outstanding inventories to hedge against price exposure. In contrast, *one-directional* markets (all buyers, no sellers, or vice versa) raise costs and risks of massive price moves.

Notes/Detail: 1. Comparing the scenarios, designation as a "market" in some cases may be misleading. 2. Even in markets with *many* independent participants as in scenario (a), a *single* ostensibly "independent" market participant such as a financial institution, hedge fund, pension fund or central bank can have an inordinately powerful impact on the market price. 3. As seen in scenario (b), high trading volume does not necessarily imply many participants as there could be countless transactions with very few participants (including computers) trading back and forth. 4. Re: terms such as "depth of the book," "spread on the bids," "painting the tape." Also refer to the topic of *price discovery*.

Price Interventions. Prices are generally dynamic, as conditions change constantly. An exception would be *price controls*, when prices are *fixed* by a policy intervention of some kind (e.g. "legal prices' or prices determined by law; re: bans; prohibition). Interference with the price of things for which there is demand give rise to distortions leading to a set of prices established "underground" in so-called *black markets*.

The "price" at which something is sold at a point in time viewed as the "high bid" for the asset/item *at that time*, but the (subsequent) high bids may fluctuate constantly depending on market conditions, meaning that some high bids may be significantly lower than other high bids at different points in time. A serious yet often unnoticed issue concerns high bids with the aid of *fiat money* and *rigged markets* (see below under Distortions and Rigged Markets).

In *goods and services* markets a system that favors the high bidder might be viewed as inherently unfair because others are unable to acquire the item; this is particularly a concern in cases of natural disasters where necessities can be in scarce supply, * and if offered, potentially at unacceptably high prices. * However, the logic usually stops there, with the solution promptly presented as some form of legal *price controls* (including *anti-price gouging* laws).

Potentially *tragically overlooked* is that if policy prevents fluctuating (including exorbitant) prices, the vital signal to *induce additional sources of supply* is cut off. When these critical price signals are outlawed, shortages can lead to devastating consequences including famine. (Also Re: Lofchie 1975; Schultz 1978; Coyne and Coyne 2015; Perry 2017; Rake 1975)

*Note: Recall the subject of *quantity* noted above and its relationship to how expensive something may be priced.

Prices can be serious affected in asset markets by regulatory moves, such as the banning of *short sales* in equities although these regulations may not be viewed as price controls per se. The regulation, however, has the effect of removing the floor at which the stocks would be bought back after being shorted, leading to potentially much more severe price drops.

Although often overlooked, a buyer of an asset bears a constant cost in the sense of *exposure to risk of loss* after purchase (hedging to reduce that exposure also involves a cost).

Distortions and Rigged Markets. As highlighted in Kennedy (2017) (Re: Subsystem 3, Col D) and briefly reviewed in Appendix 4, high bids can be the result of an *asymmetric wealth advantage* in which those with ready access to fiat money are able to outbid others to acquire real goods. When markets are *rigged/controlled* in some way then the cost/loss may be shifted to someone else; pricing shifts away from an *economic basis* and towards a policy and/or political decision-making basis (meaning usually someone including institutions are given the arbitrary power to decide). This can involve a number of policies that "protect" certain favored interests, including bailouts, loan guarantees and debt forgiveness, and subsidies for losses incurred (Re: corporate welfare). Although not obvious, non-economic sources of power include *monetary policy* which can be viewed as a potentially strong external force in the pricing of assets. Identifying the source of rigging and market distortions is not always evident and may require considerable analysis.

Fundamentals: Examples

There are many possible candidates for fundamentals (the denominator). One point which should be clarified immediately is that *rising prices* should not be confused with *fundamentals*: For example, when the prices of real estate, stocks, crypto-assets, etc. rise, often the price rise *alone* is taken to be a sign of increasing "value" and a signal to buy. There may be legitimate for why the price is rising, but these reasons are generally based in *fundamentals*, not the price rise itself. A few examples of common fundamentals of, (or measures believed to be related to price or value) are enumerated below.

1.Measures based on earnings (net profit) and earnings *growth* (e.g. the "E' in P/E ratio, PEG ratio); margin-adjusted earnings; forward earnings (Normalized); trailing 12 months earnings (ttm); earnings *yield* as in the earnings-to-price ratio, or defined by *EBIT/Enterprise Value* of a firm (Greenblatt 2006); GAAP and non-GAAP earnings; prior record earnings; forward operating earnings; Shiller CAPE (cyclically-adjusted price-earnings ratio); earnings growth (for the price-earnings growth ratio).

2.Dividends and dividend growth-based (dividend discount model, Gordon 1962; also re: investing literature, Graham 1949: 127-133; Dorsey 1994; Lichtenfeld 2015; Peters 2008, 2016); however, the commentary on dividends in the next section raises the point that dividends themselves have underlying fundamentals;

3. Company revenues and revenue growth measures;

4.Balance sheet measures of value of the firm (book value, price-to-book, etc.);

5. Perceived or real risks that are viewed as fundamental, such as *debt levels* and *debt serviceability* measures. Even if profitable, companies with heavy debt loads and increasing difficulty servicing their debts may suffer decreases in value as a result. *Counterparty risk* can also be a factor leading to price differences between assets with identical cash flows (Liu and Wu 2017).
Public finance also can be viewed as playing a key role in the fundamental value of assets. The financing of government expenditures is based on a mix of taxes, bond financing and high-powered money (aka base money) (Christ 1968, 1979; Re: *government budget restraint*); this mix can affect *real* bond values adjusted for *inflation*. For example, tax policy changes such as tax cuts *without corresponding cuts in government expenditures* may be regarded as "bond unfriendly" because rising deficits and debt/GDP ratios point to deficit financing with an increased *supply* of bonds* and *inflationary* base money. In contrast, policies that increase deficits can be regarded as *bullish* (positive) for assets outside of the bond space such as *equities* (i.e. the stock market) and real estate, to the extent that additional money creation* makes its way into those assets.
*Notes: 1. Increased supply of bonds on the bond market suggests lower prices for the bonds; see the comments on supply and demand below; an interesting historical note that provides a counterexample concerns the deficit financing during the Reagan administration's first term: The radical interest rate "reset" under

Fed Chairman Volker in effect raised the attractiveness of buying (newly issued) bonds, helping finance the deficits. 2. The money creation can include base money plus any additional money created by banking system lending on top of the base money (Re: *reserves expansion, fractional reserve banking*).

6. For firms with no earnings or losses, other metrics such as *daily average users* (DAUs), *user growth* and *monetization rates per user, user engagement metrics*, etc. may also be utilized, such as in the social media space;

7. Measures of firm cash flow, including *operating cash flow*, and *free cash flow* (FCF). A fundamental variable from Kennedy (2016) is the *rate of return on cost* (RRC); an overview of this measure is provided in the next section below;

8. It is recognized that not all fundamentals are observable, at least initially, or even quantifiable. Corporate insiders or persons intimately associated with firms may have insights into businesses that will not be reflected in the financial and other data to which analysts have access. Rumors may surface from unknown sources that may have basis in reality. Therefore, although not necessarily thought of as a fundamental itself, various *unquantifiable* and *unobservable* sources information may be essential in assessing the fundamentals of the company. Lastly, to this paragraph might be added "castles in the air" that might be thought of as intangible *imagined* fundamentals that will drive the stock higher (Malkiel 2016).

9. For so-called *crypto-assets /currencies* it can be argued that a basis for value can be found not only as a real-world means of payment* and in the *blockchain* technology, but also in *Metcalf's Law* and *network effects* where value is added as the network of users grows, in addition to the lowering of transaction costs on a global scale, portability and fungibility. While many agree that a crypto bubble is in progress, this may be a bubble with different and as-yet poorly understood fundamentals. The crypto-currency

monetary policy governing digital coin supply and limitations on growth and quantity may appear to add value through *scarcity* (e.g. Bitcoin maximum coinage to be 21 million). Moreover, when coupled with network effects (recall the discussion on price *and quantity* above), the ability to infinitesimally divide an asset into smaller quantities may also appear to add value when the prices of the individual tiny quantities are summed to make up a *unit price.*

The fundamentals may become clearer when each coin is viewed as a "brand" with competitive advantages/disadvantages over the others such as lower transaction fees, faster transaction times, ease of convertibility to fiat and other cryptocurrencies, access to highly-demanded products, programming and content (the 2017 *Cryptokitties* experiment on the Ethereum platform is only an early example) and job growth paid in that digital currency.

The ability to tie assets, contracts, and earnings to crypto-currency (Re: *smart contracts*) may be increasingly capable of delivering value to users of a cryptocurrency. Currently, since there are typically no underlying *earnings* associated with such assets, (small) pieces of the assets must be sold to generate fiat currency to pay bills (at present). It is recognized that everything may change once people can eventually pay all their bills in crypto-currency, or can convert to fiat almost with minimal cost; with smart contracts a crypto-asset might even earn an income for the holder while simultaneously serving as a means of payment to pay bills. (Re: Tapscott 2016; Antonopolous 2017).

The risks of the crypto-space must be emphasized due to a host of issues including fraud, theft, hacking* and unconfirmed activity,* lack of (commodity or other) backing in most cases, and the likelihood of many digital currencies/alt-coin values becoming worthless. (Re: Clayton, SEC Public Statement, 2017; Russo 2017; Spitznagel 2017)

It can also be argued that traditional fiat money creation through banking systems on a worldwide scale may in part be a fuel for bubbles and volatility in crypto (and other markets). Future regulatory actions can have different potential impacts, and depend on the kind taken: Outright *bans* of crypto-assets and exchanges can greatly impact price movements and volatility, while well-designed regulatory guidelines and swift and just action against unscrupulous actors, fraud and theft in the crypto-space can also serve to improve trust and stability.

*Notes:
For example, due to the risk of a 51% attack (in which the attacker has >50% of the total hash rate), *fully-validating nodes* are highly recommended since many standard Simplified Payment Verification (SPV) wallets are "...vulnerable and can be fooled into receiving fake bitcoins." (Gulbransen, 2017). Also of concern are rising unconfirmed transaction counts (Re: *mempool)*.

10. In the real estate fixer-upper example of the subjective value discussion above, the value assigned to the fixer-upper home by the second individual was based on an assumed fundamental source of value: The *estimated or forecasted profit* (surplus) that they could earn (Selling price less costs). This is a real estate version of #1 above where the term *profit* is used rather than *earnings*--both indicate a *net surplus/net benefit* after costs are covered from sales/revenues. Moreover, the profit is projected based on projected costs of repair and remodeling.

11. **Factors underlying supply and demand**: Changes in supply and demand are universally recognized as drivers of *prices*. However, this is different from being a *fundamental source of value*. Changes in supply and demand* are typically based on *underlying reasons*; recall the point made at the beginning of this section that price rises *alone* are not viewed as fundamentals. Consider a simple example of precious metals such gold and silver. Their industrial and ornamental uses may initially be regarded as fundamental sources of value that drive demand; further analysis suggests that industrial uses are predicated on profitability of the productive activity for which gold or silver are being used; if that activity ceases to be profitable then the industrial demand dries up. Therefore, the underlying source of value is some measure of *profitability* which relates back to #1, #7 and #10 above.

*Notes/Detail: Recall that demand and supply curves link *price* to a *quantity* over a given *time period*. "Changes in supply and demand" refer to a *shift* of the entire supply and demand curves. "Changes in price" can be due to a variety of factors; when the price of something changes (for whatever reason, including changes in supply and demand), the quantity sold/bought is expected to change (with some exceptions re: *Giffen goods* as they become more expensive). Returning to the example of precious metals, prices can change due to countless factors including transitory or secular changes in taste. technology, taxation or regulatory regimes, *supply shocks* from purchases or sales of gold by large buyers such as central banks, investors or discoveries of new sources of supply. The logic for *price declines* (assume that supply remains constant), is provided here: **Price Decline Scenarios** (1) Demand Side. A shift in tastes, tax or regulatory change that reduces demand for gold (i.e. the demand curve shifts to the left): The price of gold declines together with a decline in the quantity of gold sold. (2) Supply Side. Due to the discovery of new mines, or technological advances that allow miners to more profitably mine gold in the same amount of time, the supply increases (i.e. the supply curve shifts to the right), the price declines while the quantity sold *increases*. (3) Price Decrease. This case involves a price reduction initiated by a seller of the product (e.g. gold jewelry) with *no change in supply or demand of gold*. In response to cheaper prices, more buyers emerge, and the *quantity* of gold sold rises.

The three price decline scenarios are summarized below showing the likely impact on *quantity sold* and *sales* (aka *revenues* which is equal to price x quantity) for a given time period.

Scenario 1: Quantity sold declines => Sales likely down (-)
Scenario 2: Quantity sold rises =>Sales stable/increase (?)
Scenario 3: Quantity sold rises =>Sales stable/increase (?)

In Scenario 1 because both the price declines and the quantity sold declines, sales are likely to have declined. In Scenarios 2 and 3, we cannot say for sure whether sales have increased from a price decline until we know the specific prices and quantities at which the goods were sold in that time period. How much the quantity changes in response to a change in price is a key factor in determining the amount of sales for the period (Re: *price elasticity* of demand).

Although beyond the scope of discussion, it should be noted that technological advances leading to *economization* of productive activity and lower prices play an essential role in economic growth and improved living standards due to declining cost of living. For additional insights, refer to Kennedy (2017). In the scenarios above, efficiencies (technical, managerial, or other) can help producers economize on costs they can remain profitable even with sluggish sales.

Say's Law is a supply/demand framework in which productive activity and supply are preconditions for consumption/demand (Hutt 1974; Say 1803; Sowell 1973). Note that many economists including Klein (1983) state an erroneous definition of Say's Law as "supply creates its own demand;" this should be restated as "one can only buy (something) with what one has produced" (Hutt 1974: 25 citing Say 1803). Relating to an early general equilibrium model (Von Neumann 1945: 3) it was noted that it is "…impossible to consume more of a good G_j in the total process than is produced."

12. Some fundamentals would be categorized as macroeconomic, such as *nominal GDP*, and possibly *corporate gross value-added.* Other possible indicators for appropriate valuations may be based on *Tobin's Q* and the *Fed Model.* The *expected returns* of an asset based on the *capital asset pricing model* (CAPM, Markowitz 1952) could also be viewed as a basis for underlying value of the asset. For a critical analysis of the model's assumptions see Taleb 2012 (also re: *Kelly criterion*); for empirical evidence on the CAPM model also see Fama and French (1993, 2004).

Additional considerations regarding fundamentals are the time frame, and the concepts of causality and correlation, briefly discussed below.

Time Frame. Fundamentals may very well be meaningless from a shorter-term perspective. Market practitioners and those intimately knowledgeable of market behavior might point out that short-term opportunities abound that may have little or no connection whatsoever to fundamentals, however defined:

"All other investment books stress the linkage between the stock and the company. Me? I stress the abject lack of short-term linkage and the opportunities that such an un-connectedness presents. While it is true that over the very, very long term –say your lifetime—stocks should indeed reflect the fundamentals, over the short term, … the fundamentals of the company play only a part in what moves a stock up or down." (Cramer 2009: 97)

Causality and Correlation. Initially the idea that there should be a relationship between an underlying fundamental variable and another variable could lead us to assume that the fundamental variable "causes" the other; however, a hypothesized relationship does not necessarily imply *causality*. While a *correlation* between two variables may very well be found (e.g. a significant nonzero *correlation coefficient* and *coefficient of determination* in a *regression analysis*), the variables may not be *consistently* correlated, and even if so, weakly correlated at best. (Spiegel, et al. 2006). This is because due to the likely ubiquity of nonlinearities in the real world and the nature of *complexity*, there are believed to be countless forces at work that could cause substantial *divergences* between the two theoretically interrelated variables (Also re: Taleb 2012; Sayama 2015).

In sum, perhaps over *extended* time periods it may not be unreasonable to assume some imperfect and inconsistent alignment between asset prices and certain measure(s) of fundamental value that reflect the "true" value, although there may be weak correlation and lack of observability.

Focus on Select Fundamentals

Three types of assumed sources of fundamental value for firms are reviewed here: Dividends (including dividend *growth*), earnings (related to P/E Ratios), and rates of return (RRC, IRR).

1. Dividends. Dividends and/or dividend growth can be viewed as drivers of value (Peters 2008, Gordon 1962, Graham (1949) 2005 Ed.: 132 (dividend record), Kennedy 2016); numerous resources exist in the investment literature and on dividend growth stocks (e.g. "dividend aristocrats", "dividend champions," etc.).

However, the *underlying capacity* of firms to pay dividends may often be given less attention and is viewed not only as more informative but essential for a full understanding of the fundamentals. The concept of *free cash flow* used in stock valuation (Re: n-Year Discount Model; Dorsey 1994), or net cash flow (NCF) (Hitchner 2011), more closely approaches the source of potential *dividend paying capacity* which was addressed in Kennedy (2014) and developed thereafter (Kennedy 2015, 2016). **Metrics.** A common dividend-related metric is the *dividend payout ratio*, which compares, on a per-share basis, earnings to dividends paid in the same fiscal year. For example, if a firm pays $1 per share in dividends, and earns $2.50 per share in that period, the dividend payout ratio is 40%. (Lichtenfeld, 2015) The inverse of this ratio is the *dividend cover* or *dividend coverage ratio*, typically defined as *net earnings after tax/dividend* (both *recurring* or *ordinary*).

Dividend coverage measures using *equity income* and actual dividends, rather than *earnings*, is viewed here as essential. This will be further discussed in the section below in rates of return.

2. Earnings (and Earnings-based Valuation: P/E Ratio, Shiller CAPE). As an example of valuation using the *price-earnings ratio* (P/E ratio), if the firm's stock is trading at $20 per share and recent earnings of the firm are $1/share, the stock's *valuation* as defined by the P/E ratio is 20. The $20 stock price is currently what the market is *pricing* or *valuing* the stock at, whether this reflects the true value or not. Often when the P/E ratio exceeds its *long-term historical average*, concerns are raised that equities are being *overvalued* (i.e. being overpriced relative to earnings). **Defining Fundamentals**. Determining whether an asset is overvalued is largely subjective and there may be no consensus due how the fundamental(s) are defined--even when there is agreement that *earnings* is a fundamental source of value, there can be marked differences of opinion or weighting. To illustrate, a stock is trading at $20/share and the firm's earnings are $1/share *this* fiscal year. This corresponds to a valuation of 20 according to the P/E ratio (=20/1). However, some analysts believe that the company's earnings could drop to 50 cents/share *next* fiscal year. Based on these poor earnings prospects, the stock might now be considered *overvalued* relative to the fundamentals as *defined as next year's earnings*.: To justify this current valuation of 20, the "correct" stock price that reflects the projected decline in earnings should therefore be \$10/share not \$20/share (20=10/0.50). At this corrected "fair value" stock price of \$10/share based on *next year's earnings*, the *valuation* of 20 is excessive and should fall to 10 when fundamentals are defined as *current year's earnings* (=10/1).

Earnings as a fundamental variable may have shortcomings as used in practice. **Per share basis (EPS)**: Since earnings are typically reported on a per share basis they can be manipulated by buying back shares, so that earnings *per share* are rising when in an absolute sense they may not be. **Cash Flow:** As detailed in Kennedy (2014), earnings are *not* a measure of cash flow. Adjustments to earnings to arrive at some equivalent of cash flow also can be inadequate and misleading (e.g. *funds flow*). Cash flow is critical because of its *physical*, not accounting, nature. Cash is used to pay dividends to investors, and to repay debt. Therefore, the focus on cash flow is preferred. *Equity income* is viewed as an essential cash flow measure detailed below.

3. Rates of Return

Rates of return are another assumed source of fundamental value. Specifically, *rate of return on cost* (RRC) and the *internal rate of return* (IRR) are the focus of this section. An analysis comparing these two rate of return measures alongside (net) earnings (=net profit) and *equity income* (both as a percentage of revenues) is also provided. First, the EPR is briefly reviewed.

EPR: Clarification. The P/E ratio was noted above; it's inverse is the *earnings-to-price ratio* (EPR) and can be viewed as a rate of return measure. However, this ratio is for an investment, not the firm itself and is typically measured on a *per-share* basis: To clarify, EPR represents a rate of return for the *investors, not of the firm itself*. Investors who purchase at a particular share price are essentially "buying" a certain amount of company earnings per share; their EPR "rate of return" can be expressed as a percentage of the cost (share price). Since the early 1980's to 2015, the cyclically-adjusted EPR declined from the 10% range to roughly less than 5% by 2015 (Kennedy 2016:80).

Firm-Specific Approach

The *rate of return* of a firm *itself* is the foundation of the *rate of return on cost* (RRC). The *internal rate of return* (IRR) can also be computed for either a firm itself or for an owned asset, although the former approach many not be common (Kennedy 2016). The *firm-specific* rate of return is distinguished from rate-of-return measures on investments or acquisition of assets. Examples include *return on investment* (ROI), *return on assets* (ROA), the IRR of an asset *owned* by a firm, * *total returns, earnings-to-price ratios* (EPR), etc. Firm-specific refers to the entity itself as a self-contained stand-alone entity that incurs ongoing costs and generates (positive, zero or negative) cash flows.

Note: *The owned asset can be a business partially or wholly-owned by the firm; the rate of return such as ROA or IRR would be based on cost of the asset.*

Overview: Rate of Return on Cost (RRC). A fundamental rate of return measure and driver of value posited in Kennedy (2016) is the *rate of return on cost* (RRC), assumed to be the long-term innate *real* rate of return of a financial entity such as a business. Here, the RRC is also viewed as a form of firm-specific *natural rate of return* (NRR), particularly when considered over sufficiently long periods of time (e.g. 10 years+). RRC is also not expressed on a per-share basis.

In Kennedy (2016), the RRC was defined as:

NNCF/Cost

…where the numerator, NNCF, is *equity income* of the firm, to be detailed further below, and *cost* is the total cash outflow in each period (typically a firm's fiscal year). NNCF and cost are *synchronous*, in the same year: In other words, RRC captures the return-to-cost relationship synchronously. It should be clarified that this "synchronization" between returns and costs should be distinguished from the Shumpeterian concept in economics where *production and consumption* in economy are viewed as synchronized, making time irrelevant. (Rothbard 1987:99)

As noted above, the RRC is considered to be more meaningful when observed over extended periods of time (10 years +). *Cost* refers to the cash outflows related to the operations of the financial entity and including capital expenditures and acquisitions occurring in the same period (e.g. fiscal year, calendar year) as the revenues generated by the entity.

RRC as a Fundamental Variable. The RRC is posited to have some fundamental relationship with the price of the asset (equities) in both an economic and financial context. This relationship is assumed to apply both to *income-producing* or *non-income producing* assets (although some complexities exist with certain non-income producing assets as addressed in Kennedy 2016).

Real vs. Nominal. In economic analysis, *nominal* rates are typically converted into *real* rates by adjusting for price changes which represent costs to consumer or producers. In contrast, the RRC is considered to be a *real* variable because the RRC already represents the relationship of *return* to the *cost* borne (in other words the cost that is associated with the return). This is a rate of return of the financial entity (e.g. the firm) *itself,* not the rate of return to the investors holding the equity of the firm, or on specific balance sheet items of the firm (e.g. ROA, ROE).

Financial and Economic Entities Concept. The framework for the understanding of *financial entities* and applies to both business entities and individuals. The focus here is on businesses (firms, companies), although individuals can have a rate of return on their *cost of living* (RRCOL). A more theoretical yet essential concept is that of an *economic* entity when the activity in which the entity is involved is considered to be *voluntary* (Kennedy 2016, citing Walker 1888)

Natural Rate of Return. To reiterate, the measure of rate of return for a financial entity *itself* is RRC (rate of return on cost) and is viewed as the firm's own innate or *natural rate of return* (NRR) over extended time periods. There are therefore countless natural rates of return in an economy.

Recall that some financial entities can have consistently *negative* RRCs which continue because they have insufficient or no *revenues* and rely upon sources of *financing* such as equity issuance, donations, taxes, or some form of obligations such as debt financing.

Detail: Equity Income (NNCF)

Equity income (abbreviated as EI), and is defined as *net net cash flow* (NNCF) which is *net cash flow less acquisitions*. EI is the numerator of the rate of return on cost (RRC). EI if stand-alone is typically expressed as a *percentage of revenues* and abbreviated as EI%.

NNCF is cash flow *net* of capital expenditures (NCF aka *free cash flow* or FCF*) with a key modification being that NCF (FCF) is further reduced by cash outflows from acquisition-related activity, intangibles and other key investments including joint-ventures (JVs) and license, patent and technology-related acquisitions (Kennedy 2014: 11; Kennedy 2016: 87-8).

*__Note__: It is recognized that FCF is a non-GAAP financial measure. Although generally FCF is defined as net cash flow after operations less capital expenditures, there may be substantial variations in use by firms.

Although dividends and dividend growth are often a focus of evaluating stocks, the underlying equity income is essential for dividend coverage and payment as well as debt service.

Equity Income in Connection with Dividends. Equity income is *potential* physical income as expressed in cash, that is attributable to equity holders of the firm regardless of *whether dividends are paid or not*, and is considered to be the primary source of the firm's capacity to pay dividends. The term "physical" is added because in contrast to "net income" or "earnings", equity income is physical in the form of *net cash flow*.

Equity Income in Connection with Debt Service (SOR). Equity income *less* dividends is viewed as the primary *source of repayment* (SOR) for debt and the basis for the evaluation of *debt service capacity* and the determination of *credit-based interest rates* (CBI) as detailed in Kennedy (2015). The following diagram shows the components and computation of SOR and the debt service coverage (DSC) ratio in a static case:

CREDIT-BASED INTEREST, FIRM-SPECIFIC		
Source of Repayment (SOR) (aka Primary Source of Repayment)	Debt Service (DS) (Principal + Interest)	Debt Service Coverage Ratio (DSC Ratio)
Net Net Cash Flow (NNCF) less: Dividends/Distributions =SOR for Debt Service	Depends on: 1. Initial Loan Amount 2. Loan Term/Amortization 3. Interest Rate	=SOR/DS
Static Example		
25	16.67	1.50
Credit-Based, Existing Debt Load	Interest rate computed based on known initial loan amt (refinance)	
Credit-Based, Natural Rate	Initial Loan Amount and Interest Rate Unknown	
Credit-based is firm-specific		

The computation of the CBI and CNRI in a static case is detailed in Part II (A.1) and Part II (A.2), respectively.

Earnings vs. Equity Income. The question might arise as to why equity income should be used rather than earnings. Some reasons are provided here.

Equity income represents a cash flow, and cash is required to pay dividends. As detailed in in Kennedy (2014) the source for the repayment of debt and for the payment of dividends ultimately is *net cash flow* (i.e. physical cash remaining after all cash costs are deducted).

Earnings is an accounting construct that does not necessarily reflect the cash flow available to meet dividend payment and debt servicing requirements. Even *funds flow* which adds non-cash depreciation to earnings, is not considered an appropriate measure of cash flow (Kennedy 2014: 4).

Earnings figures may also be somewhat easier to manipulate as they are typically reported on a per share basis which can be subject to manipulation through share buybacks and other creative accounting approaches (Kennedy 2014: 12). Equity income figures do not adjust for shares. Also, the SOR (equity income less dividends) figure for debt service capacity is computed by deducted *actual* dividends, not on a per-share basis.

Revenue Growth and Equity Income. The growth of revenues also should be given consideration in the analysis of equity income since equity income is typically shown as a percentage of revenues. A particular situation which we wish to capture is when declining revenues are coupled with a declining equity income percentage of revenues. This area was not specifically addressed in Kennedy (2014), but is explored here in the section on *double declines*.

Internal Rate of Return (IRR)

An alternative measure of rate of return called the *internal rate of return* (IRR) relates subsequent returns to an initial cost *over time*, rather than synchronously. The IRR computes the rate of return such that the initial cost outlay (IC, which is an outflow) is incurred in an initial period followed by a future stream of cash flows. In a process referred to as *discounting* or *discounted cash flow analysis*, the IRR is the rate computed by iteration when the future stream of cash flows* is equalized to the initial cost:

$$NCF_1/(1+r) + NCF_2/(1+r^2) + \ldots + NCF_n/(1+r^n) = IC$$

*In this example the cash flow stream is defined as the NCF_t for a business *this future stream could also be in the form of future cost savings* [Kennedy 2016:45; IRR employing historical financial data with NNCF (i.e. equity income) was presented in 52:56)].

This internal rate of return may go by various names, but all which link rates of return *to time* whether or not debt may be involved: The *discount rate, yield-to-maturity* (YTM) on bonds, *time preference rate* or *interest rate for time*. It should be clarified that in this sense, interest is not limited to debt, but is a form of return: "Hence, time-preference and interest income exist…not simply as a charge on loans but as a return earned by every investing capitalist" (Rothbard 1987: 99).

Firm-Specific IRR. An example that computes IRR with historical financial data for a firm was presented in Kennedy

(2016: 53-55). Limitations in the use of the IRR for firms in this way were also detailed. The initial cost was defined as all costs incurred by the firm in the initial year (i.e. payments to all factors including labor and capital investment in that fiscal year); the subsequent *net cash inflows* are defined as annual revenues less costs; the IRR computation covers a defined time period (e.g. 10 years, 7 years). The computed IRR was a *rate of return* (or *rate of discount*) to the firm that treated *time* as a resource (*interest rate for time* or *rate of time-preference)* in that other (physical) resources were given up *initially* in the hopes of *future* returns. The relevance of that exercise to the *Bohm-Bawerkian* or *Austrian concept* should be highlighted, that is: "...the concept of time and time-preference in the process of production." And: "...(T)he capitalist, for his service of supplying factors with *present* goods and waiting for *future* returns, is paid the discount (Rothbard 1987, Note 4); italics added. (Also Re: Bohm-Bawerk 1901)

Comparing Fundamental Variables

The question of how various potential measures of fundamental value compare was explored in Kennedy (2016) for three variables: net profits (earnings), IRR*, and RRC. Below is an updated table that adds in the *equity income* percentage of revenues (EI%). The net profit figures are also as a percentage of revenues and are not on a per-share basis (nor are any of the other variables).

*Note that to compute a *firm-specific* IRR over an extended time period in Kennedy (2016), the firm's financial data were grouped into 10-year sets. Each dataset (referred to as "sets") consisted of sequential 10-year periods shifted by one year. Since there are not enough 10-year sets to bring the computation to the most current year, a forecasted version (labelled "F") of IRR was constructed to include the final 10 years (based on historical trends) to render the observation periods comparable among the variables.

As seen in the chart, IRR and RRC have very roughly similar means and standard deviations. Their means tend to be lower than that of net profits with more variability, and perhaps can be seen as a more conservative measure in this sense. Equity income's mean is the lowest, with variability in between that of NP% and the other variables. In sum: 1. RRC appears to exhibit more volatility than profitability; 2. IRR (without forecast) may be a reasonably intermediate measure between RRC and net profit. As previously noted, a major shortcoming of the IRR is that when using 10-year periods a *forecast* is necessary to bring the values to a more current period.

Table: Descriptive Statistics for Fundamental Variables

COMPARISONS	NP %	NP%	RRC	IRR (F)*	IRR	EI %
Mean	17.4%	18.2%	14.5%	13.4%	14.2%	12.3%
Standard Deviation	4.5%	4.3%	7.3%	6.0%	6.5%	5.6%
Observation Period	83-2016	88-2016	88-2016	88-2016	88-2006	88-2016
Notes: NP%=net profit/revenues; (F) includes forecast; EI% = equity income/revenues						

Notes

1. The years are fiscal years which are also calendar years.
2. Distributions were fitted for the entire sample of the variables. None of the variables appeared to conform to a normal distribution based on goodness-of-fit rankings (the highest rank for a fitted normal distribution was #6 for one variable: EI% per the A-D test). Fitted results were as follows for each variable:

NP% (1988-2016): Pearson6;
RRC (1988-2016) Dagum (4P), Johnson SB *both* highly ranked;
IRR (without forecast) (1988-2006): Frechet (3P);
EI% (1988-2016): Dagum(4P), Johnson SB *both* highly ranked.
Parameter estimates are not shown. Further details on distribution fitting are in **Appendix 2**.

3. Standard errors for each of the variables were as follows: NP% (1983-2016): 0.0079; NP% (1988-2016): 0.0082; RRC (1988-2016) 0.0138; IRR(F) (1988-2016):0.011; IRR (1988-2006): 0.015; EI% (1988-2016): 0.011.

Regression Estimates

In addition to comparison of key variables with descriptive statistics, regression analysis (*ordinary least squares* or OLS) was conducted to determine any significant relationships between the candidates for fundamental variables (NP%, IRR, RRC, EI%). The results are presented in three rows: In the top row are the

116

estimated equations with their parameter estimates; in the second row are the computed *t-statistics* for those parameters, and in the bottom row are the *adjusted R-squared (Radj)* and *F-statistic*. Very simplistically stated, higher values suggest greater significance, or in the case of the *Radj,* a stronger potential relationship. For purposes of brevity, results deemed insignificant are simply stated as such.

The shortcomings of regression analysis, the assumption of linearity and reliance on small samples are recognized (Paulos 1990; Spiegel, et al. 2006). Moreover, *ordinary least squares* (OLS) as an estimation method employed here leads to inconsistent and biased estimates of the coefficients (Pindyck and Rubinfeld 1991:350). The risks of drawing conclusions based on econometric models that employ regression equations should also be highlighted (Re: Leamer 1983).

Case 1. RRC as a predictor of IRR (i.e. IRR as the dependent variable). The forecasted data of IRR is excluded so that only the actual figures are used. The sample period is therefore 1988-2006 18 observations, no forecasted observations for IRR). The regression estimate suggests a somewhat significant, positive relationship between the two variables; however, a weak significance of the constant may affect any presumed relationship between the variables:

$$IRR = 0.046 + 0.697RRC$$
$$(2.57) (6.24)$$
$$Radj = .697 \qquad F = 38.9$$

Case 2. RRC as a Predictor of Net Profit Percentage (i.e. net profit as the dependent variable; sample period 1988-2016, 28 observations). No significant relationship was found.

Case 3. Net Income as a Predictor of Equity Income (i.e. equity income as the dependent variable; both variables are as a percentage of revenues; sample period 1988-2016; 28 observations). No significant relationship was found.

Case 4. Net Profit as a Predictor of IRR (i.e. IRR is the dependent variable, sample period is 1988-2006, 18 observations). The estimate suggests a non-significant or very weak relationship.

Firm-specific RRC and IRR can always be computed and compared on an ongoing basis, alongside net earnings which is clearly the most commonly used measure. Based on this analysis, the RRC is a reasonable proxy for IRR and is preferred for use with datasets consisting of multi-year subsamples (e.g. 10-year sets), given the IRR's limitations as previously noted. RRC data covering extended periods of time are preferred to capture more reliable measures of firm-specific rates of return.

APPENDIX 3. Relative Frequency Distributions:
A Dynamic View

This appendix presents histograms that show the *relative frequency distributions* of each of the 10-year subsamples of the five variables EI, RRC, RRCG, SPG and REVG. The 10-year subsamples are sequential and shifted by one year (e.g. Set 1 corresponds to the 10-year period 2016-2007, Set 2 to 2015-2006, and so on, until the last 10-year period obtainable from the entire sample of each variable). For further details on the variables, datasets and fitted distributions, see Appendix 1.

Relative frequency distributions can also be referred to as *empirical probability distributions* "(S)ince relative frequencies can be thought of as empirical probabilities…" (Spiegel, et al. 2006: 169). Estimates of probability were originally defined by a concept of *frequency* assuming sufficiently large samples (von Mises 1964) followed by an axiomatic approach (Kolmogorov, 1933) due to the difficulty in defining "sufficiently large." The small samples of this study are recognized as a shortcoming.

Static and Dynamic Approaches. A relative frequency distribution for an *entire sample* of each variable only gives a single "snapshot" of the variable over the observation period and does not capture the *movement* of empirical probabilities over that time period. The dynamic approach attempted here presents histograms for the 10-year sequential sets for each of the five variables studied beginning with Set 1 (2016-2007), followed by Set 2 (2015-2006), Set 3 (2014-2005), etc., generated in spreadsheets. The variables are EI, RRC, RRCG, SPG and REVG, in vertical order; each variable's histogram is positioned so that it can be viewed in sequence horizontally when the pages are turned, in the hopes of helping identify any patterns of movement over time with a "flip book" format; note that the hoped-for visual effect may not be successful in printed format. For details on each variable, see Appendix 2.

EI

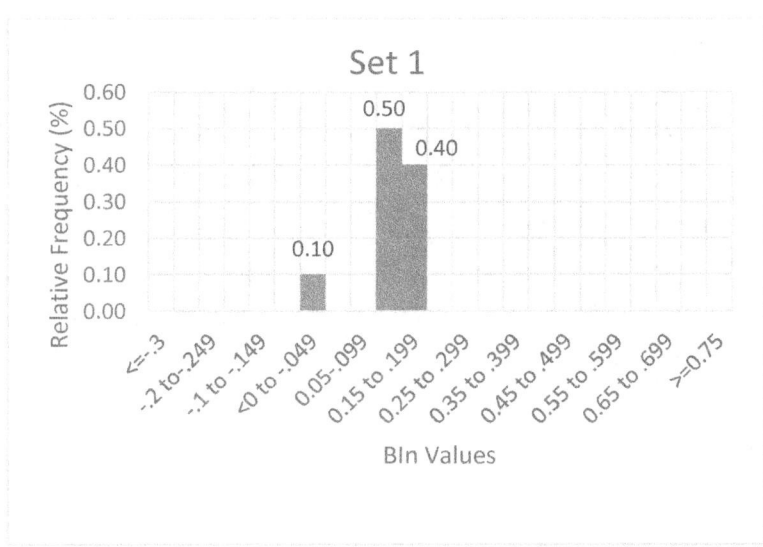

RRC

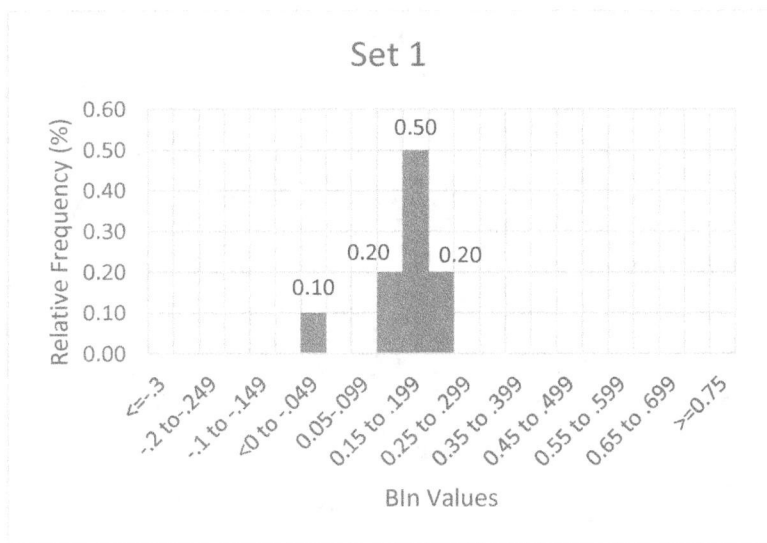

RRCG

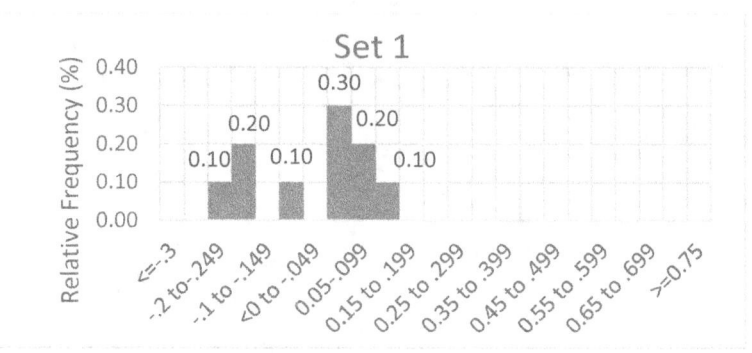

SPG

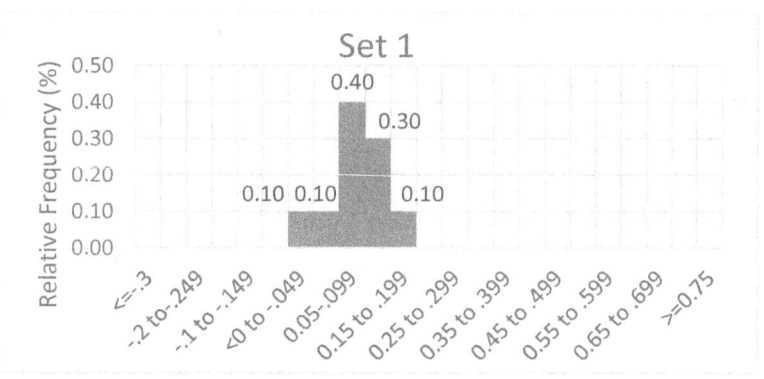

REVG

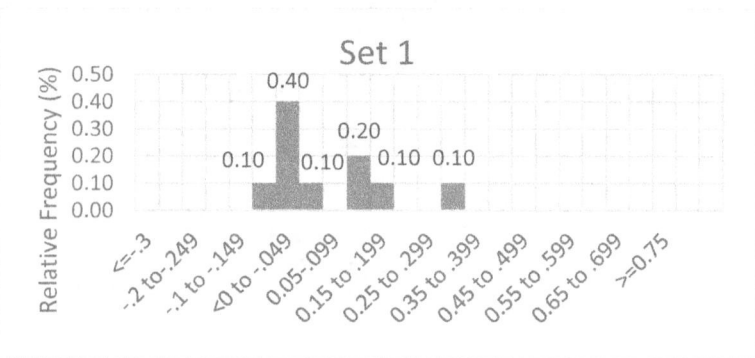

EI

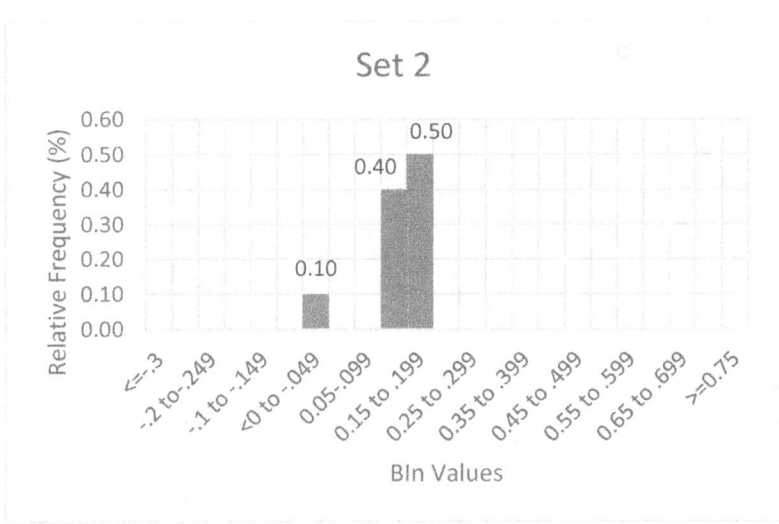

RRC

RRCG

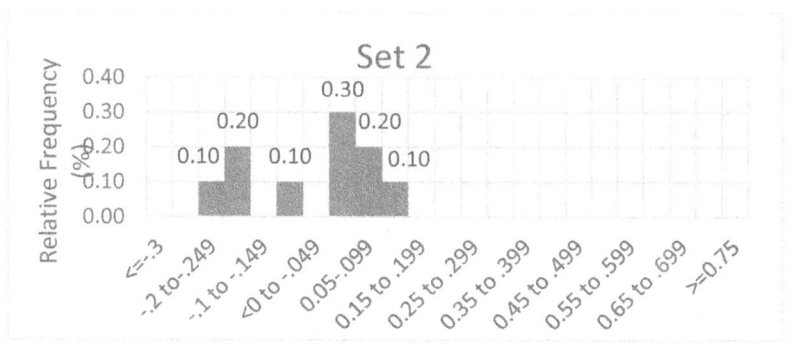

SPG

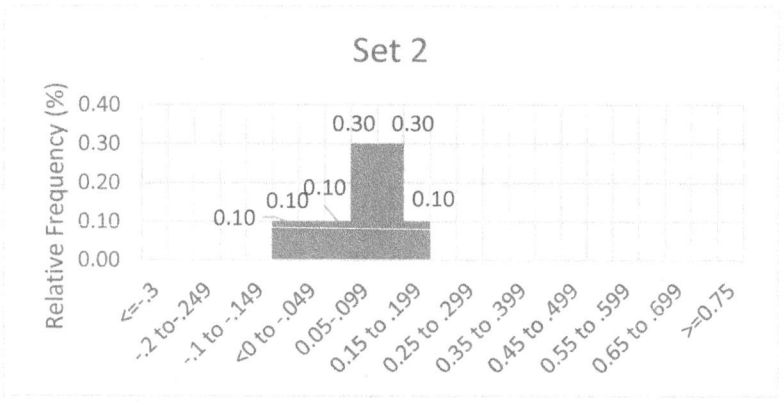

REVG

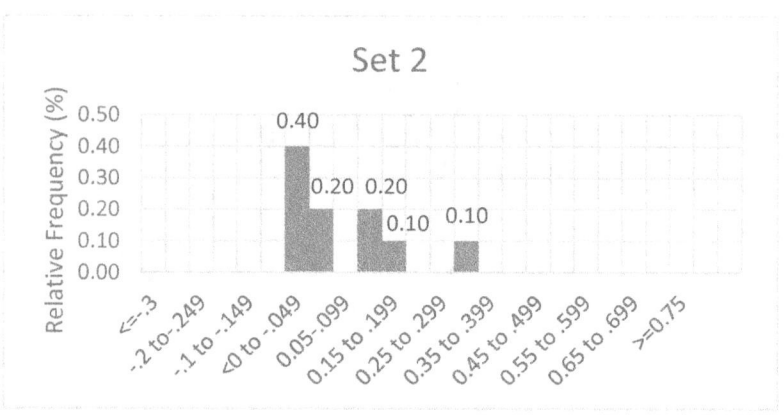

EI

RRC

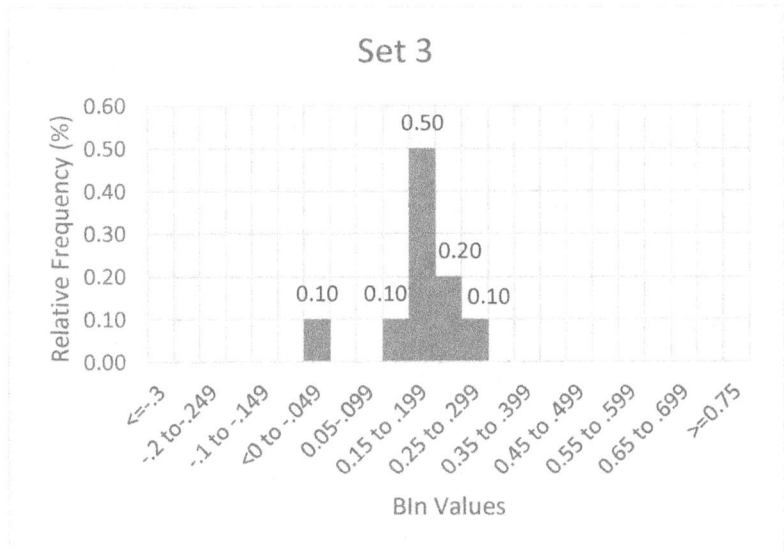

RRCG

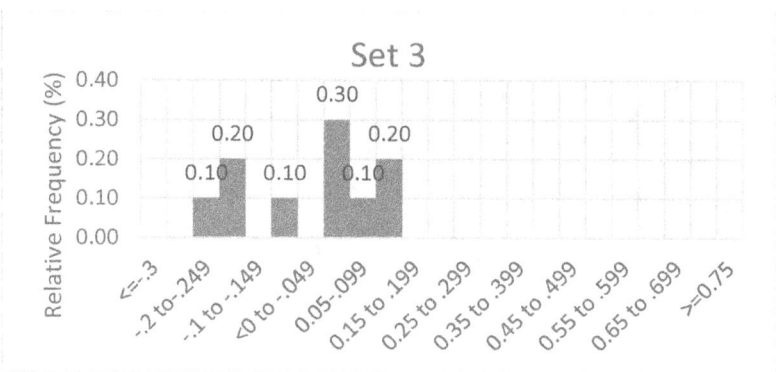

SPG

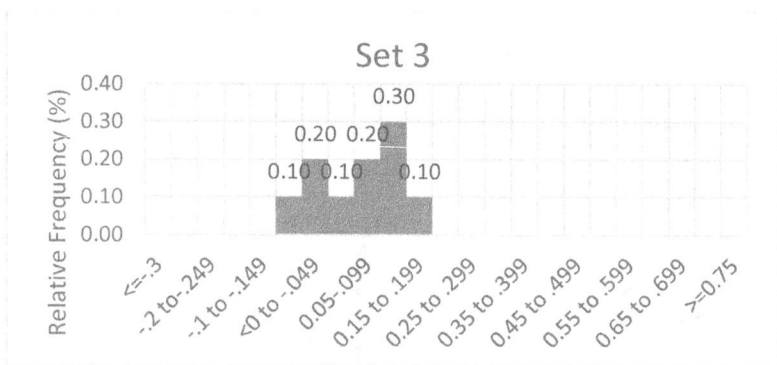

REVG

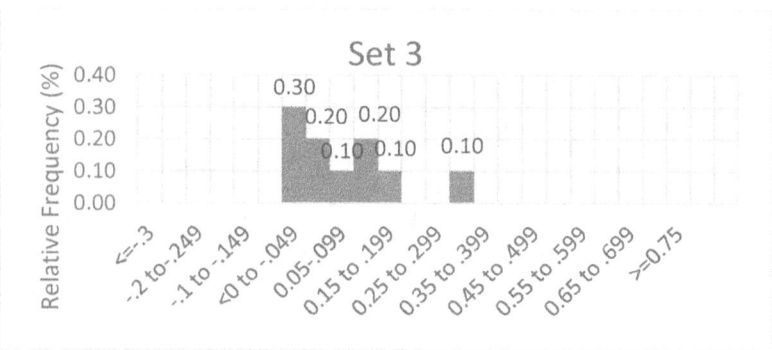

125

EI

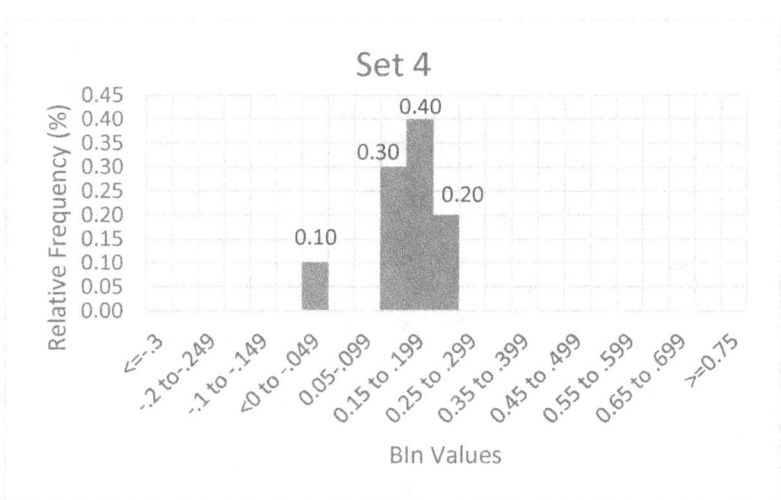

RRC

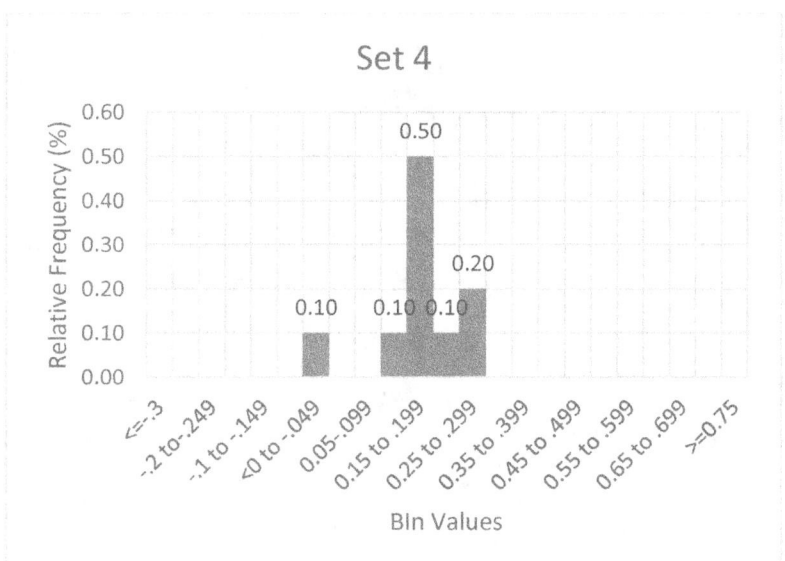

RRCG

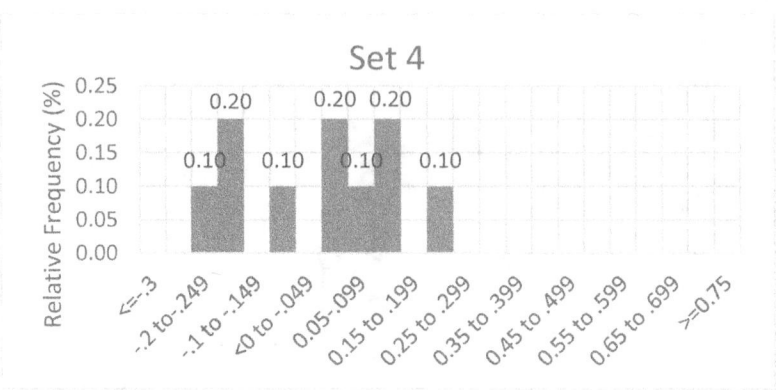

SPG

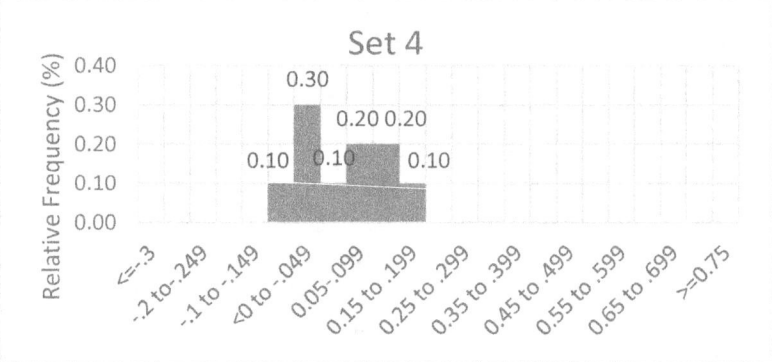

REVG

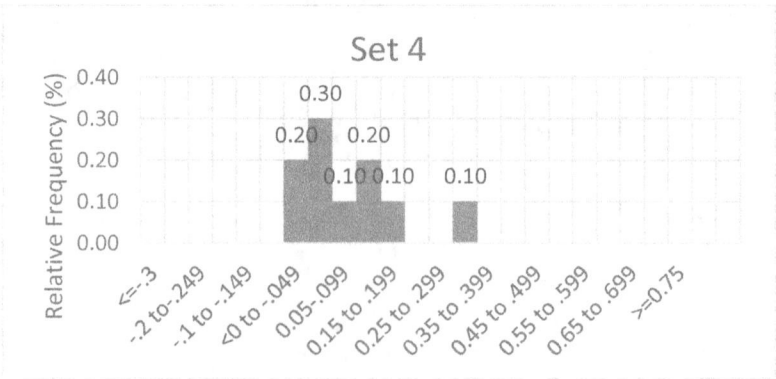

EI

RRC

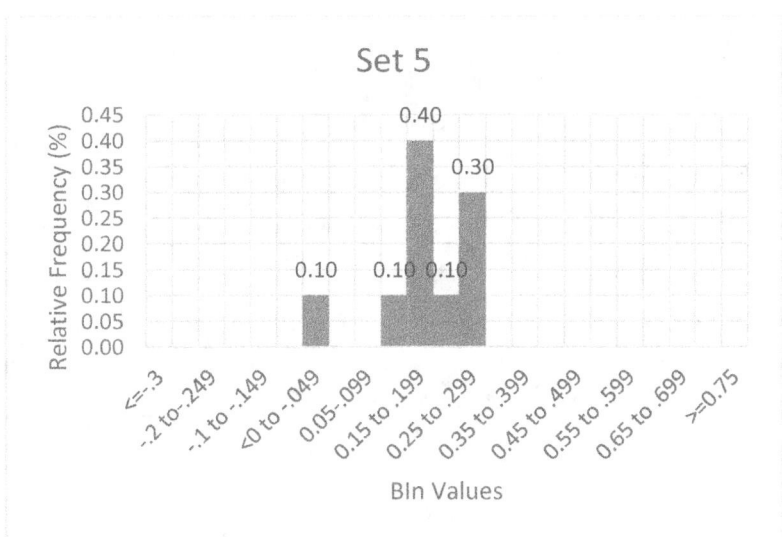

RRCG

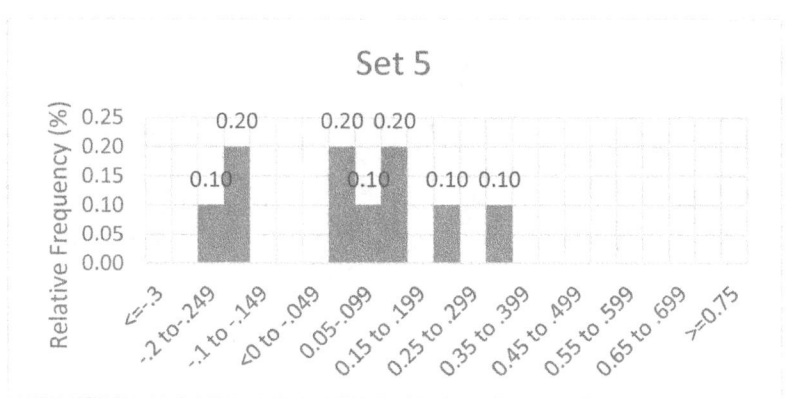

SPG

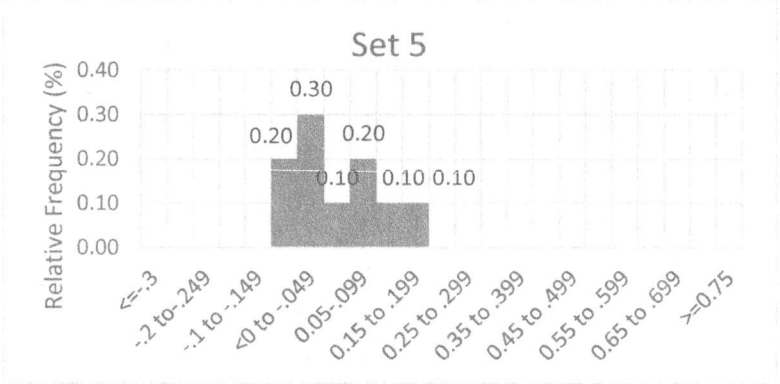

REVG

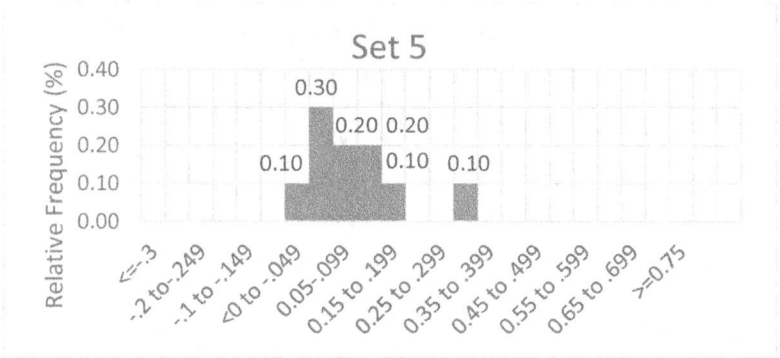

EI

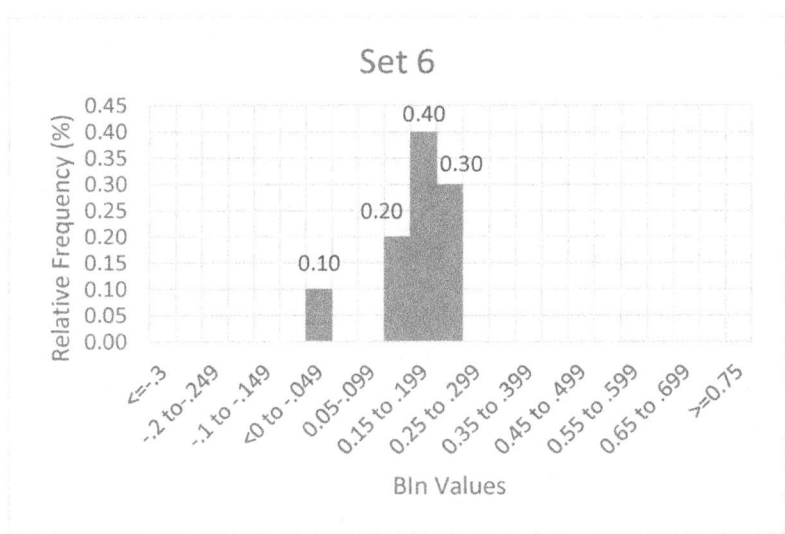

RRC

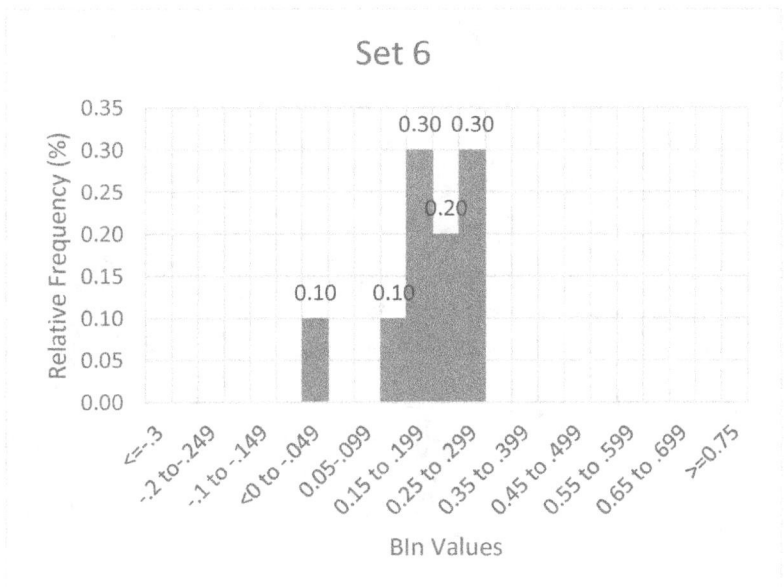

RRCG

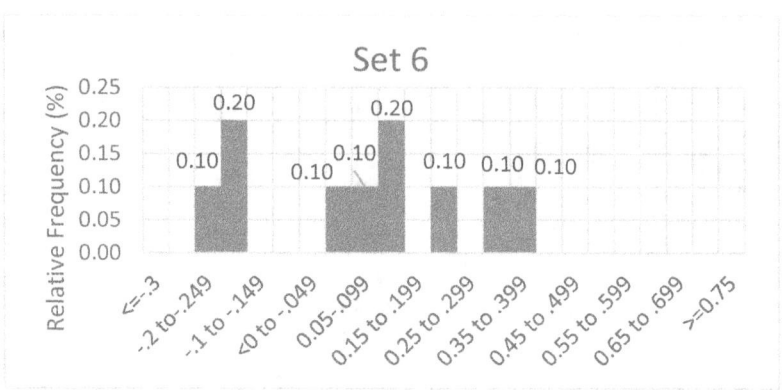

SPG

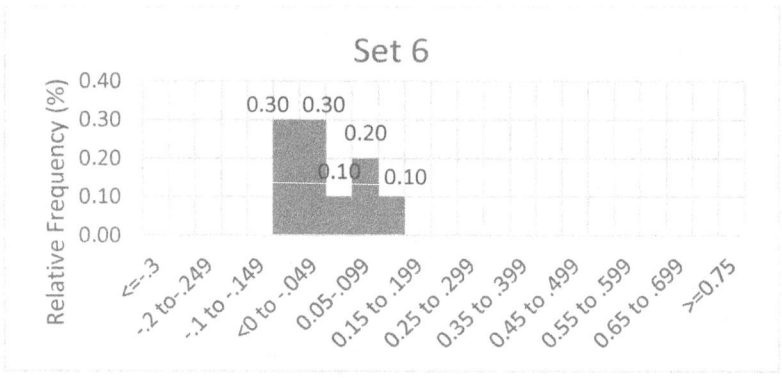

REVG

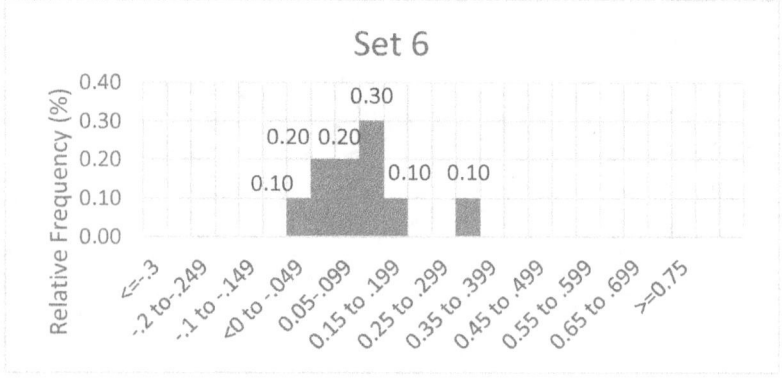

131

EI

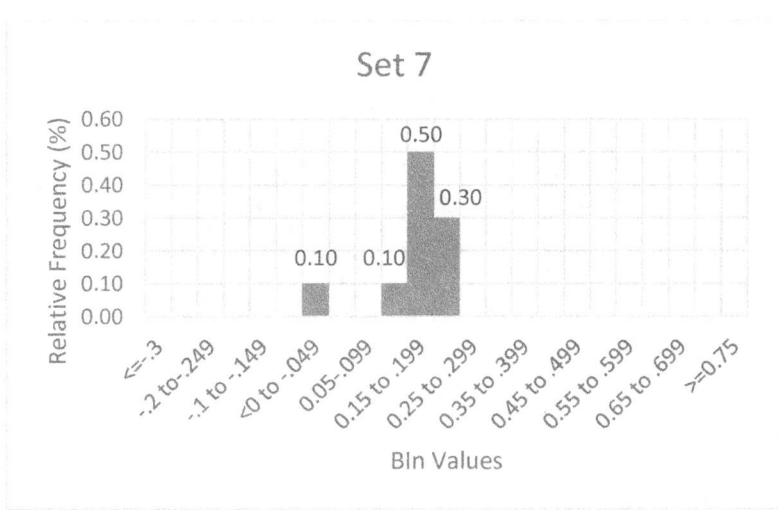

RRC

RRCG

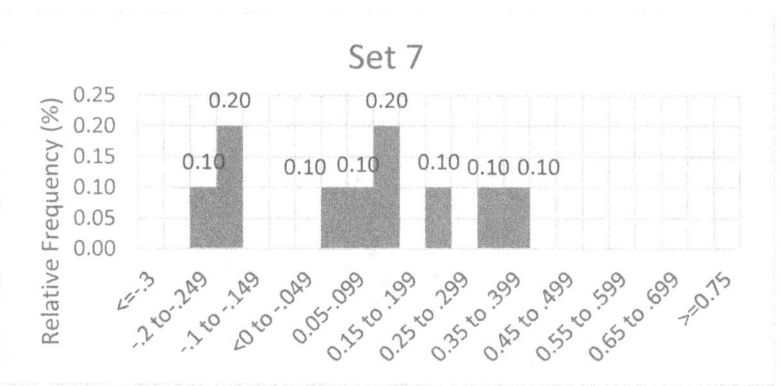

SPG

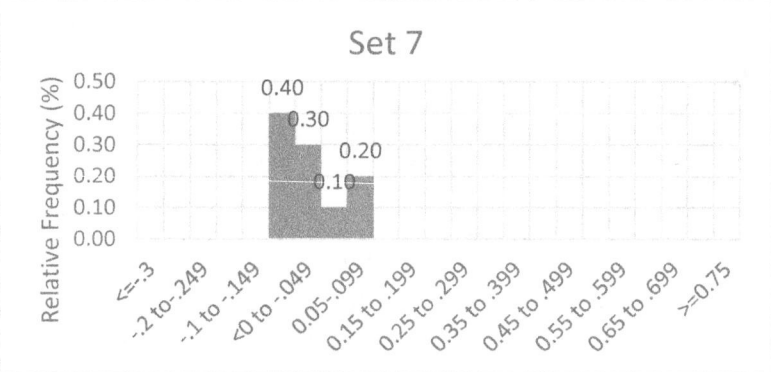

REVG

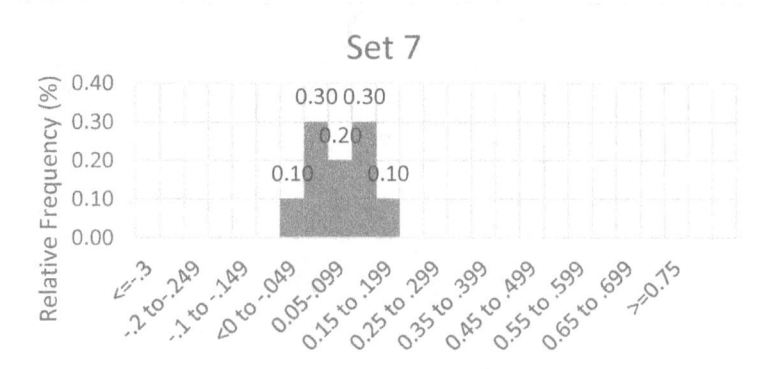

EI

RRC

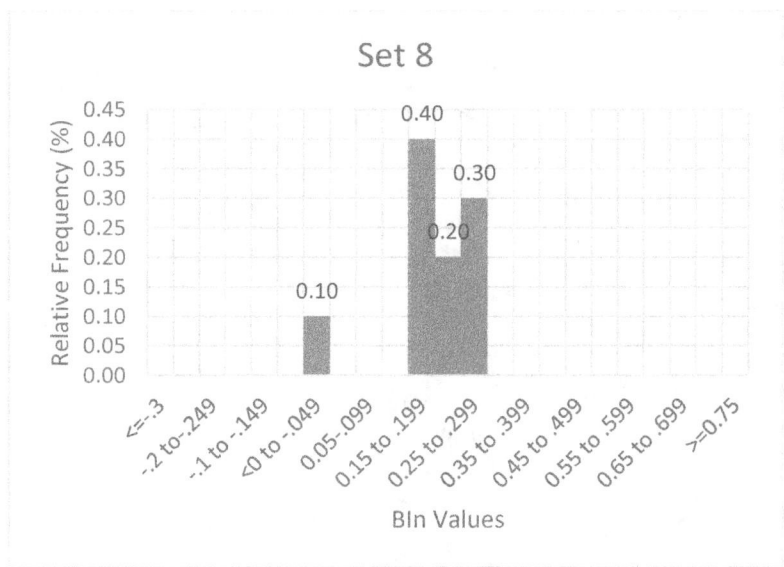

RRCG

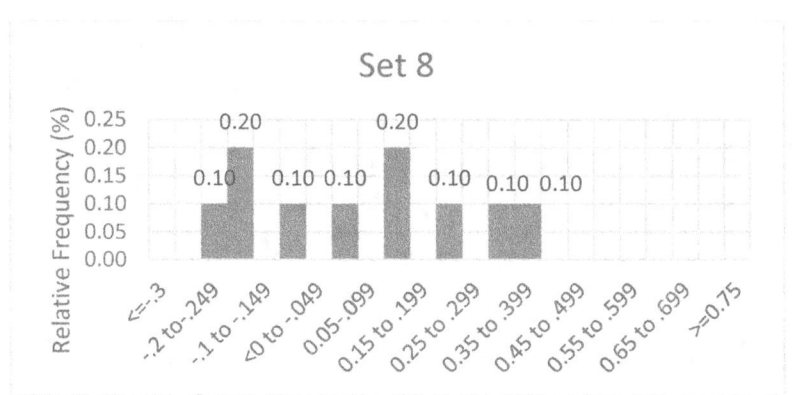

SPG

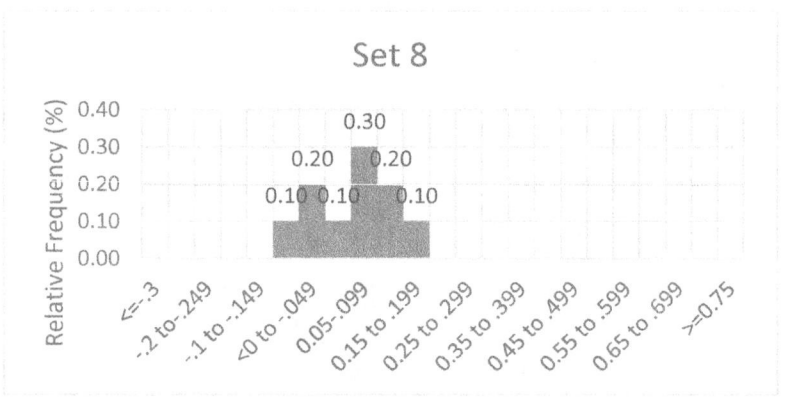

REVG

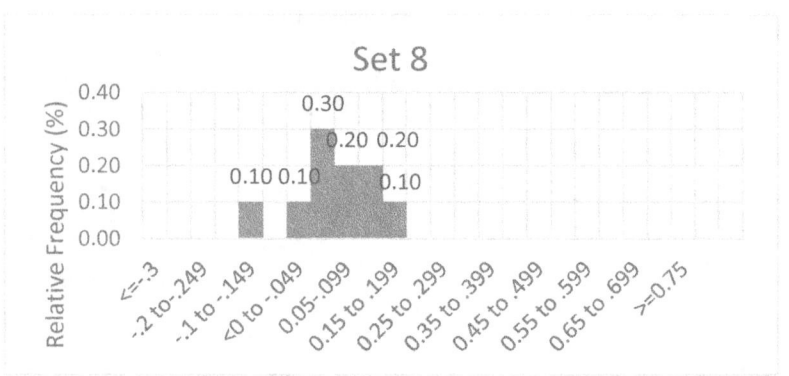

EI

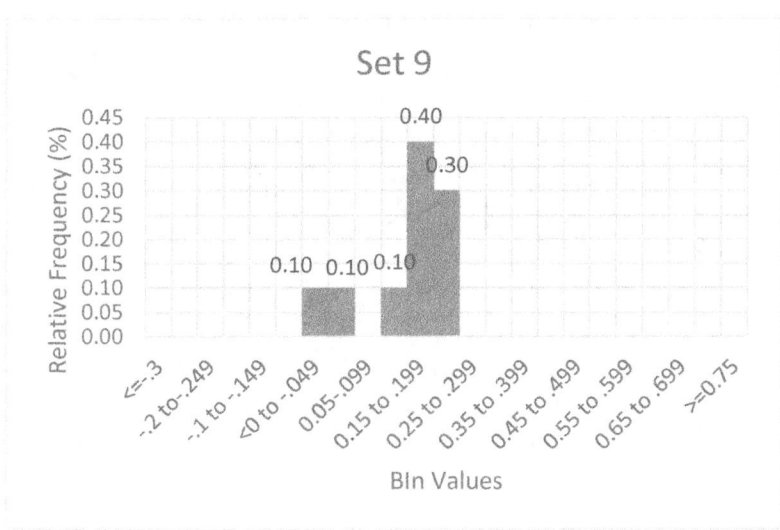

RRC

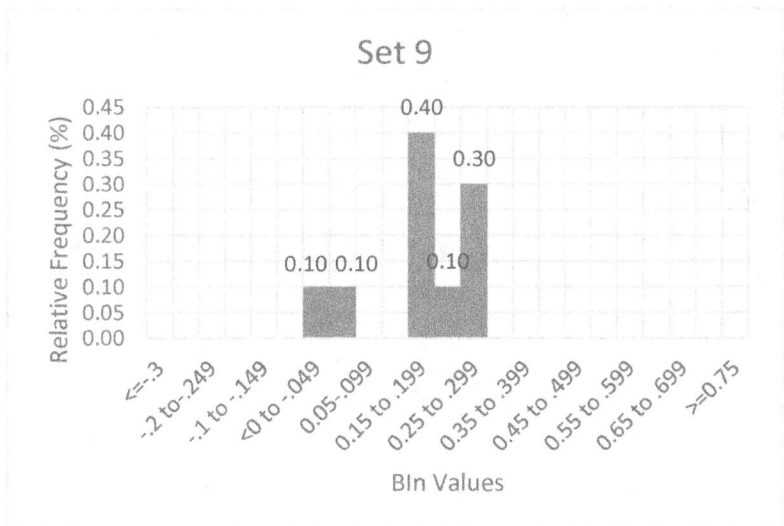

RRCG

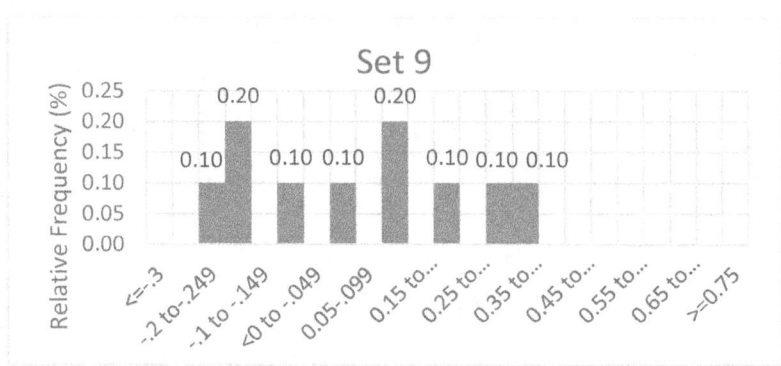

SPG

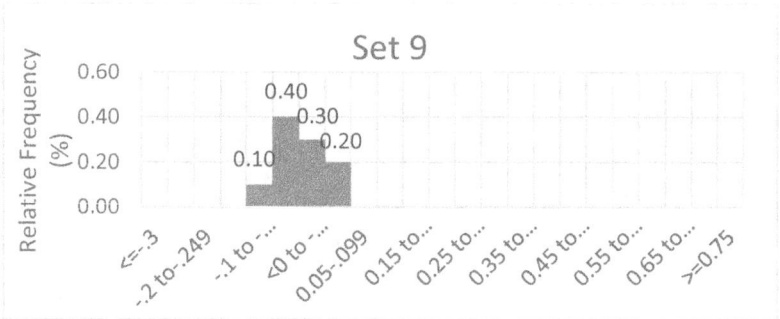

REVG

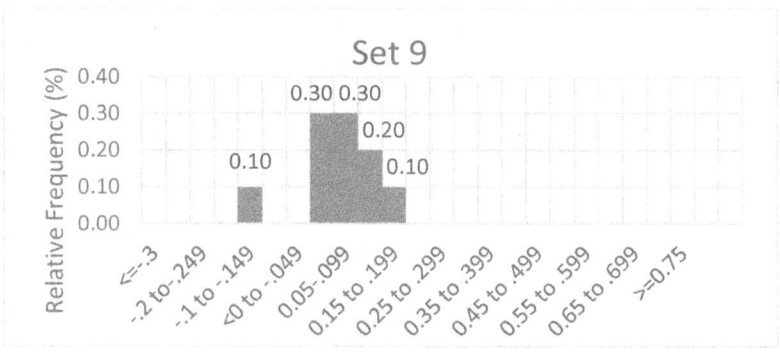

EI

RRC

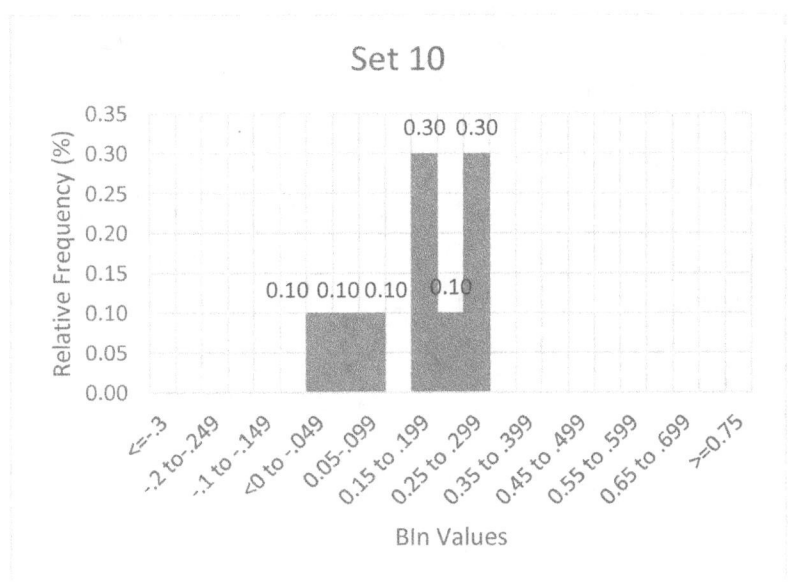

RRCG

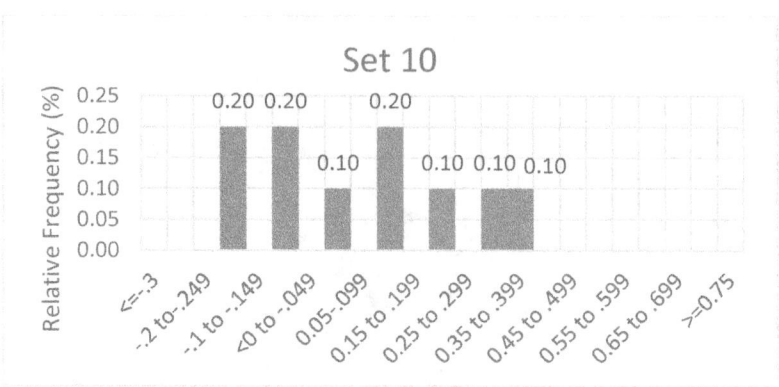

SPG

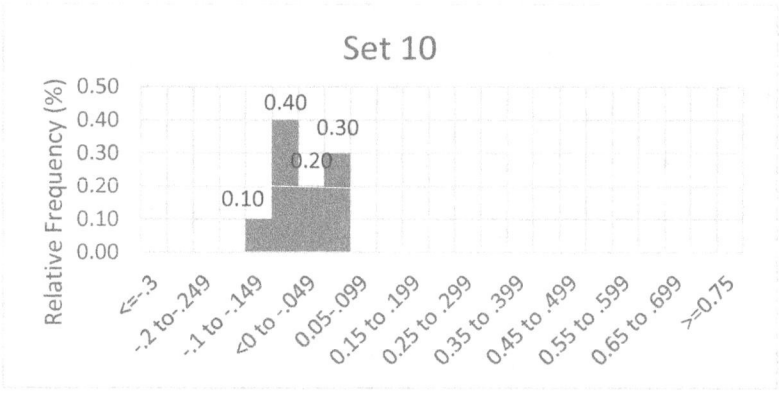

REVG

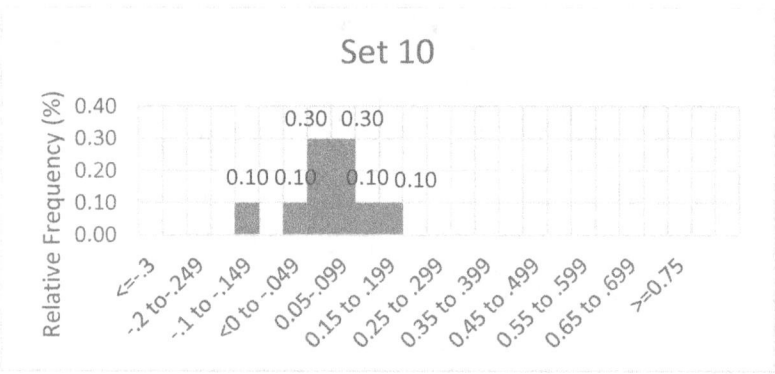

EI

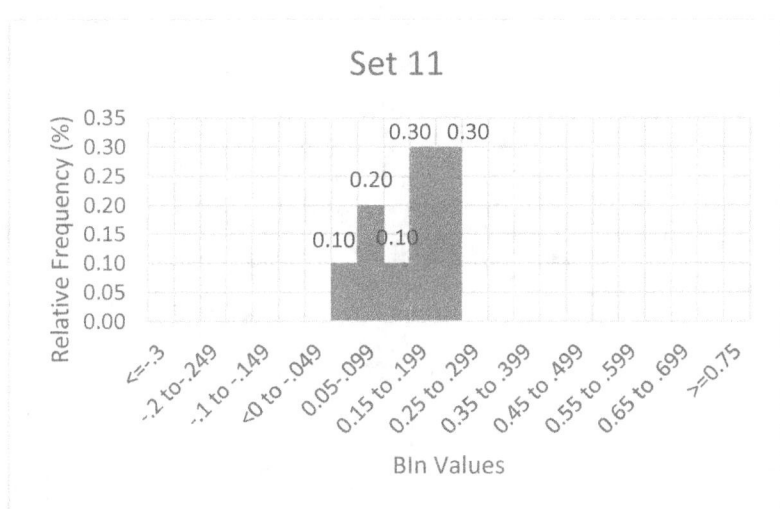

RRC

RRCG

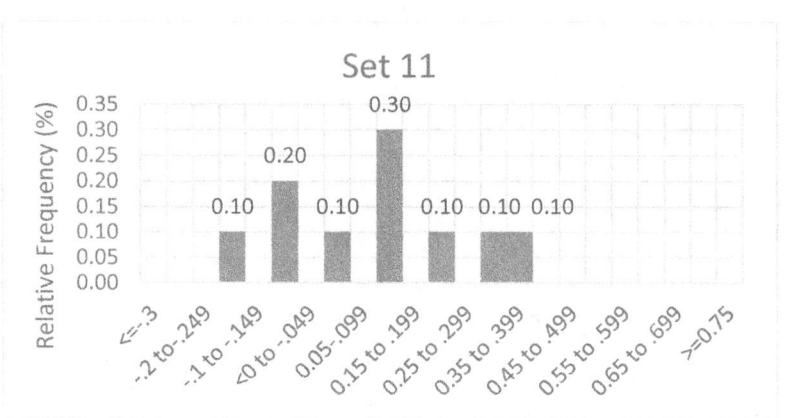

SPG

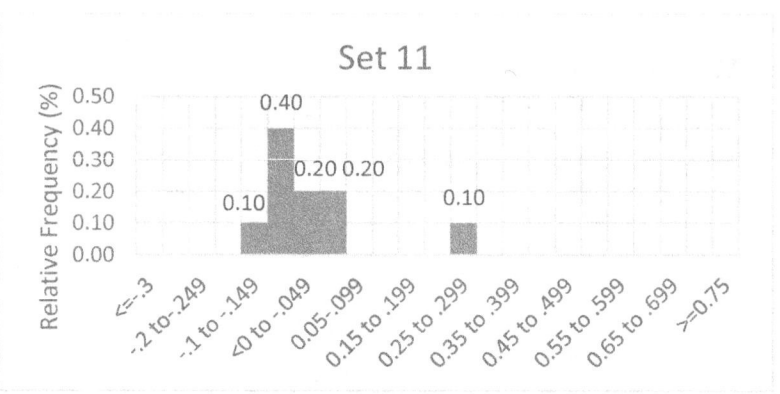

REVG

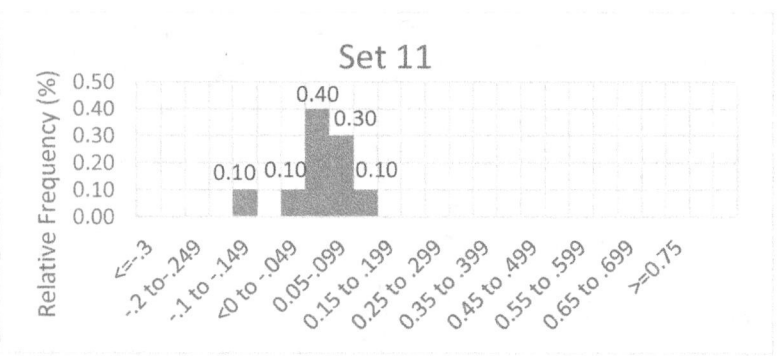

EI

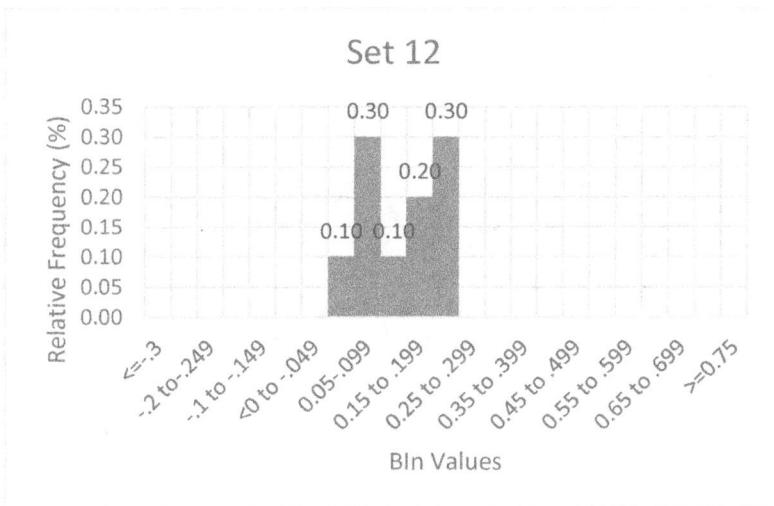

RRC

RRCG

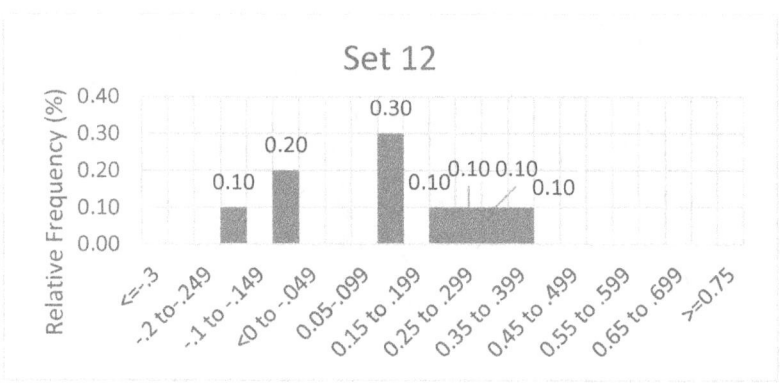

SPG

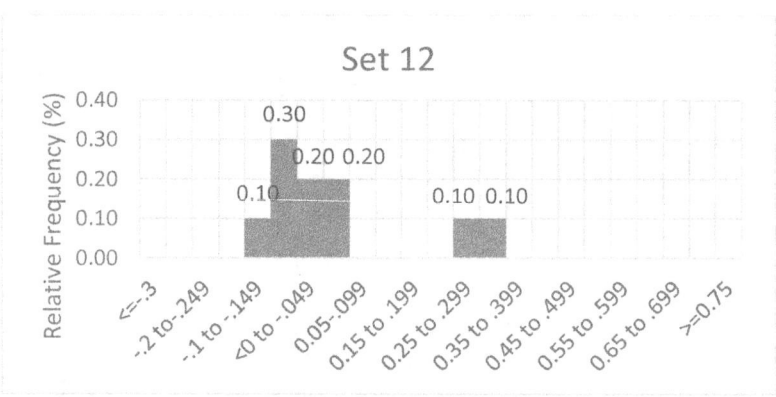

REVG

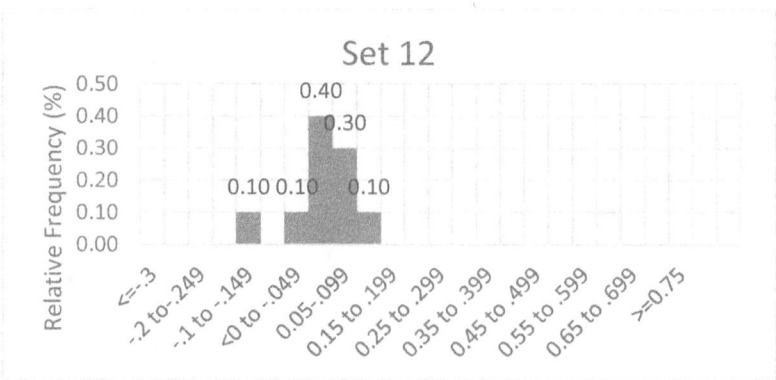

EI

RRC

RRCG

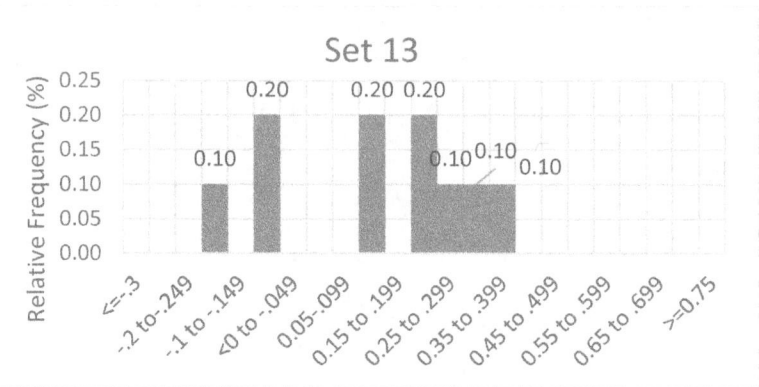

SPG

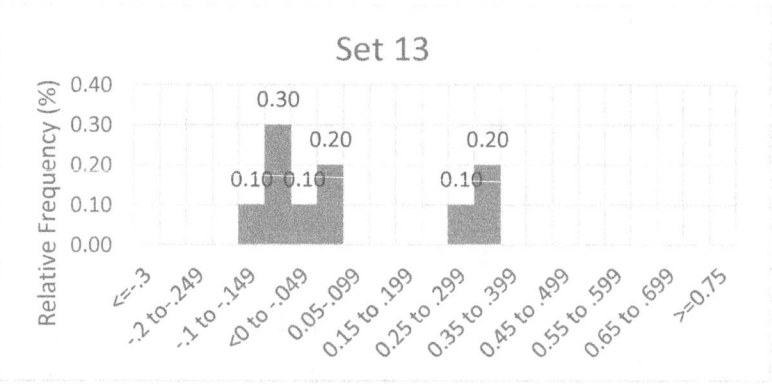

REVG

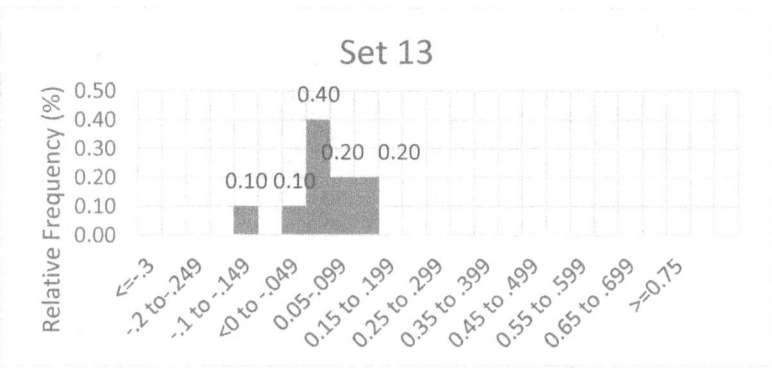

EI

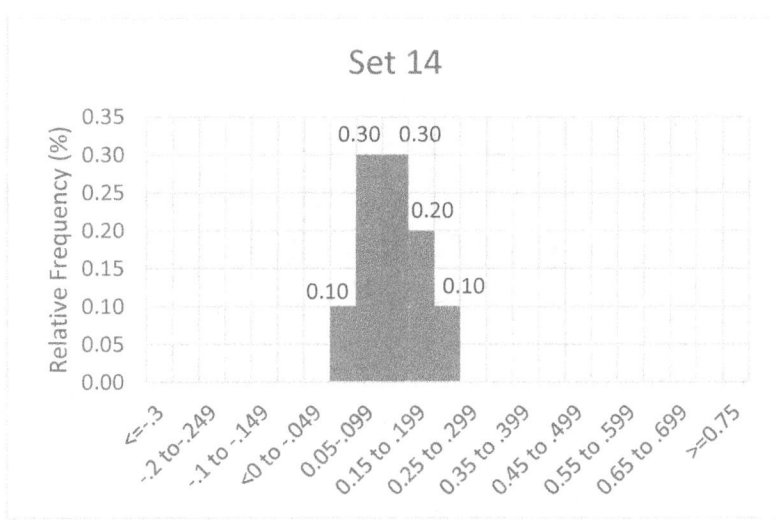

RRC

RRCG

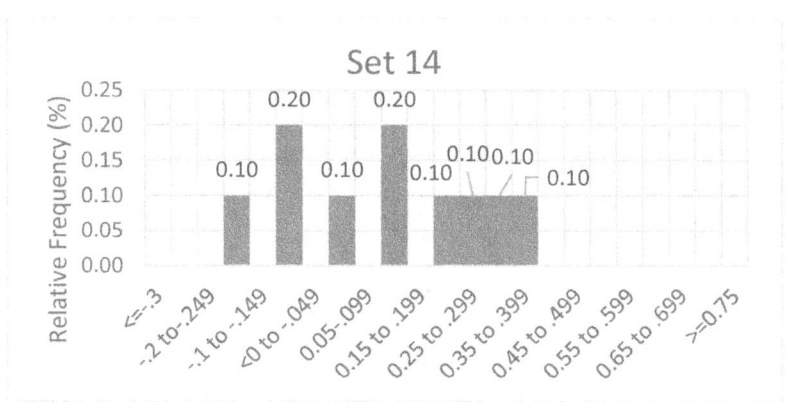

SPG

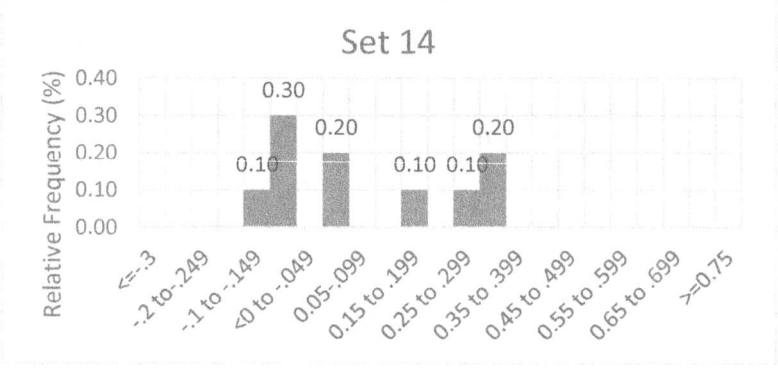

REVG

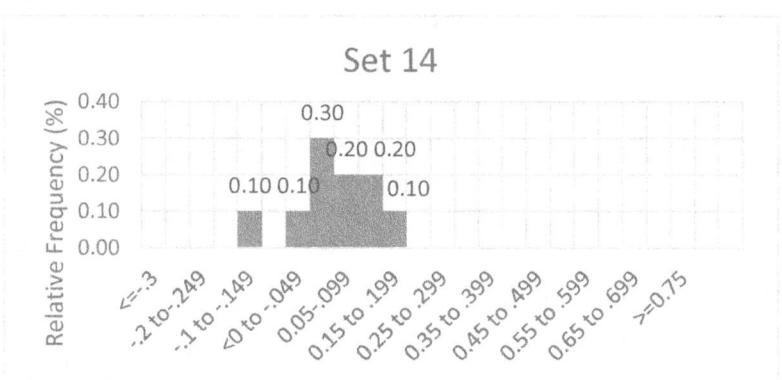

EI

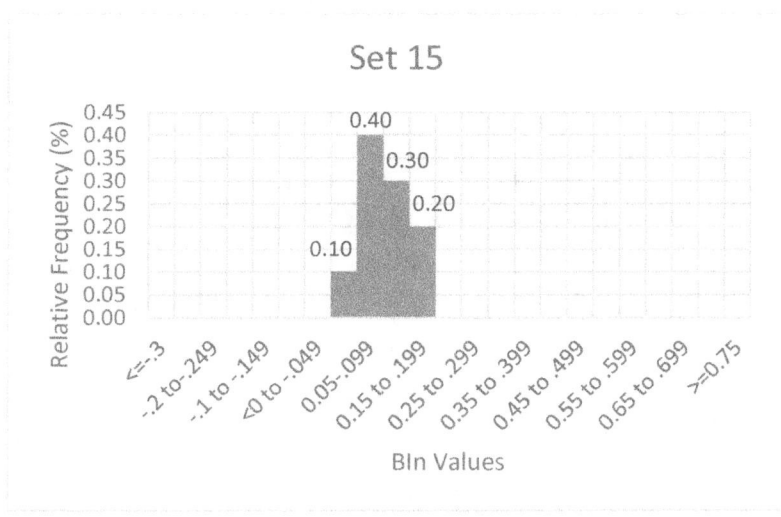

RRC

RRCG

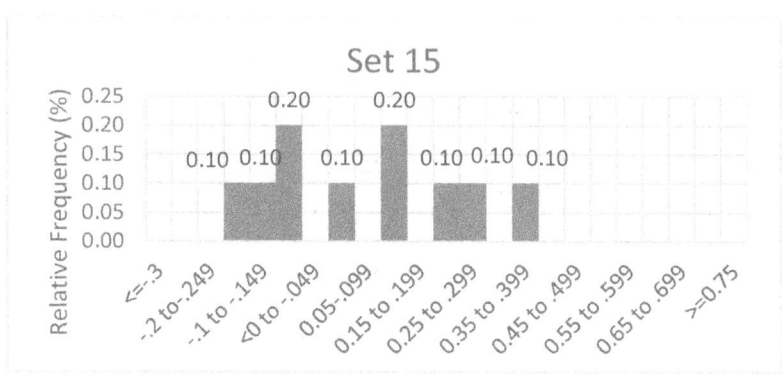

SPG

REVG

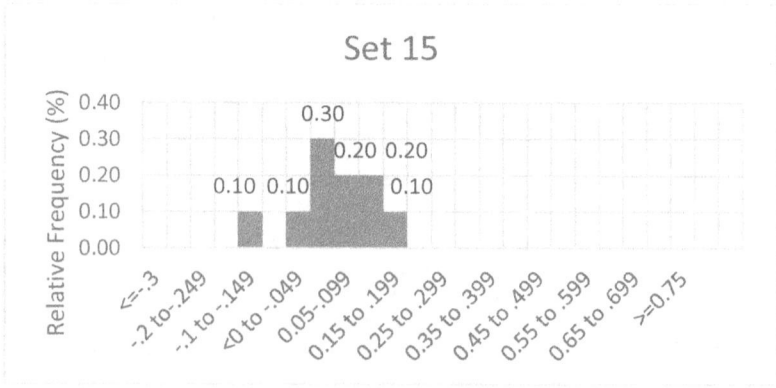

149

EI

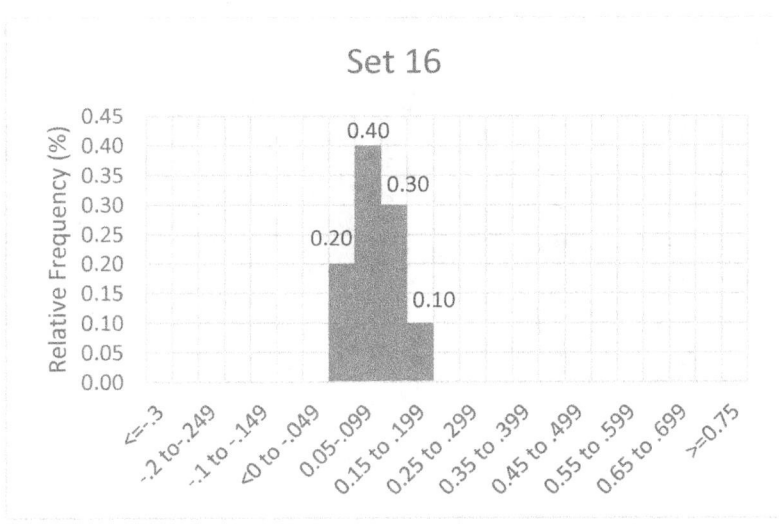

RRC

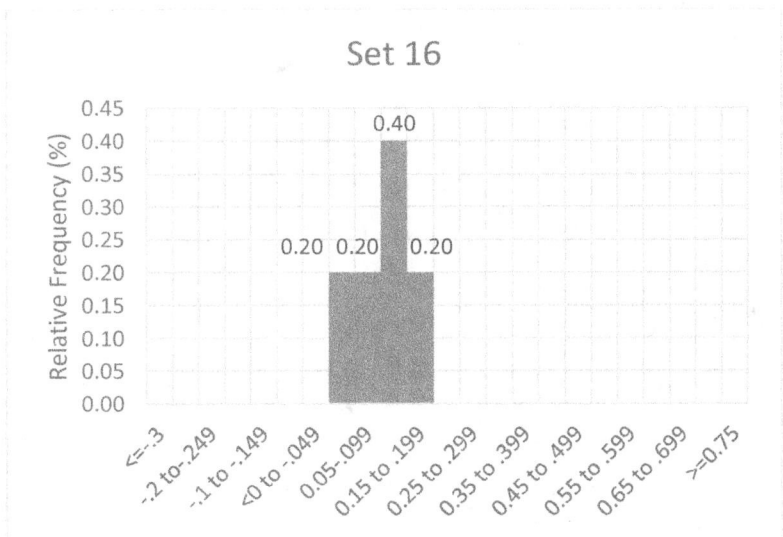

RRCG

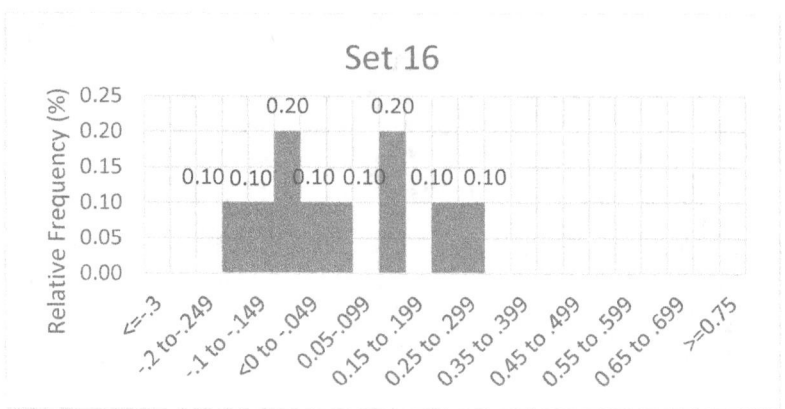

SPG

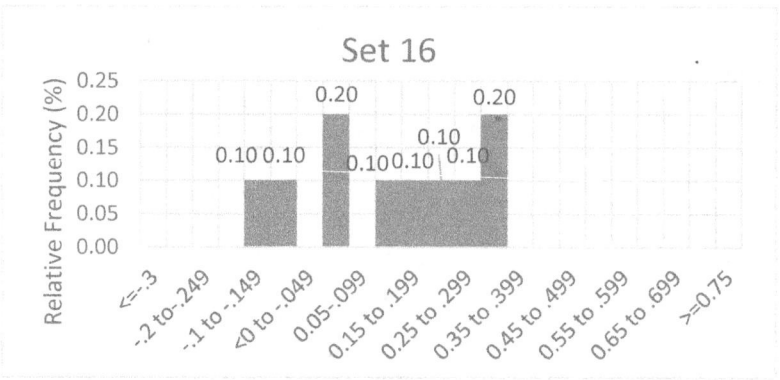

REVG

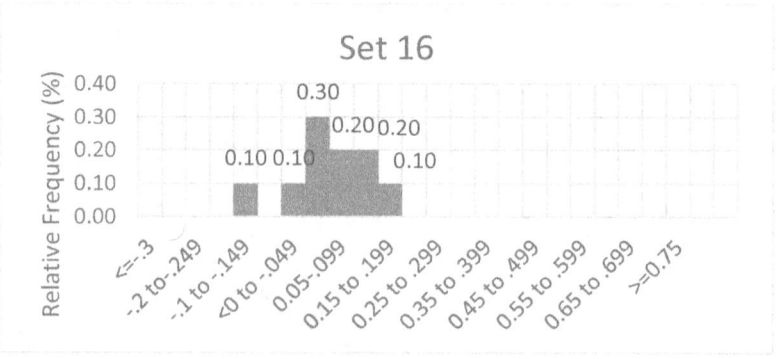

APPENDIX 4. Policy and System Dynamics Overview

The Policy Table below is reproduced from *Economic Distortion Dynamics* (Kennedy 2017) and refers to "Subsystem 3" policies that relate to the financial and monetary system. Subsystem 3 is a fiat monetary and financial system that is viewed as a natural extension of System 2's reinforcing feedback loop towards expanding need for inflows. As expenditures exceed income, *income-based* inflows (i.e. taxes) may fall short. Fiat money through the financial system and central banking apparatus is a supplemental source of financing that can be called upon to provide additional inflows to continue the operations of System 2.

Subsystem 3 Policy Table. The policy table summarizes the characteristics of Subsystem 3. The table is organized in rows and columns. The rows corresponding to *policy interventions* using notations such as **Sub3.1** which indicates "*Subsystem 3 policy #1.*" The columns (A through N, abbreviated "*Col*") describe characteristics, potential outcomes, and phases (initial, overshoot, reversal) of each policy as follows: Policy intervention type (Col A), level/scale of the policy (Col B), rhetorical justification for the policy (Col C), and the *transfer of wealth* (beneficiaries and cost-bearers) in columns D and E, respectively. Columns F through J are possible outcomes during the initial phase (Phase 1) of the policy's feedback loop. Column K represents the "Overshoot" phase marked by an unsustainable point of high deficits/debts, and expenditures exceeding inflows. Columns L through M represent a *reversal* (or possibly an *S-Curve* or outright *collapse* of a system), in which secondary policies are implemented and invasive actions are taken to "fix" the problems caused by the initial policy intervention. This phase may also be marked by significant social unrest.

Key features of wealth transfer and phases are noted here:

It should be emphasized that an important distinction between a fiat-based money and money backed by a *real asset* (such as gold, silver, or other assets) is that fiat money gives the owner an *asymmetric wealth advantage* (**Col D**), as unbacked fiat money can be used to acquire and accumulate *real assets*.

Col E: The costs are borne by those who hold the fiat currency as a form of savings over time. Because additional fiat money creation dilutes the currency, there is a likelihood of a decline in *purchasing power* (Re: inflation) of goods and services. (This fiat money asymmetry is also relevant to fiat money cryptocurrencies covered in **Sub3.6b.**)

However, despite the ability to create unlimited quantities of fiat money, at least in theory, Subsystem 3 has systemic limitations; the aftermath of an *overshoot* (**Sub3 Col K**) the reversal phase (**Col L** through **Col N**) can in extreme cases morph into a collapse, in which defaults may be inevitable.

First, this can occur because the accumulated debt is large enough that *debt service* and full repayment become problematic; at the national level, these include *obligations* such as the unfunded liabilities of government-run pension systems to pensioners, or medical coverage for seniors (e.g. Medicare in the U.S.) (Re: pensions/social security U.S.: Mitchell 2017; Re: *fiscal gap*; *fiscal crisis*; Alesina, et al., 2013; Kotlikoff 2015, McKinsey 2015). Concerns about the role of existing financial institutions, future directions and threats to the monetary system have also been highlighted (El Erian 2016; Rickards 2017).

Second, at a subsequent point in the feedback loop following the overshoot, the quantity of money-printing required to cover all the obligations may be insufficient due to the risk of a high or even a *hyperinflation*; in extreme cases hyperinflations can reduce the value of the money to near zero (as can be evidenced by newly-issued bank notes of extremely large denominations (e.g. Zimbabwe; Venezuela: See Gupta, Hanke 2017).

III. OVERRIDING INTERVENTIONS with FIAT MONEY FINANCING (Re: Monetary policy with fractional reserve banking)

Sub3.#	A. POLICY INTERVENTION TYPE	B. Level/Scale (primary)	C. Rhetorical Justification	D. Decoupling: Returns portion. Wealth gains via political support. (Income/wealth distorted upwards)	E. Decoupling : Cost portion. Cost-Bearers: bearing the cost (Net incomes/wealth reduced)
Sub3.1	Reduction of Borrowing Costs (re: financial repression)	National	Growth/stability	Borrowers	Savers, Lenders
	a. Interest Rate Decoupling (gap)	Supranational		Asset holders	Job seekers
Sub3.2	Compensation to Financial Institutions		Growth/stability	Financial system	Savers
	a. Lending cost reduction policy			Lenders/financial	Holders of currency
	b. Fractional Reserves and Expansion Legality			Banking system	
	c. Caps on deposit rates			Banking system	Savers
	d. Loan guarantees		Growth/stability	Financial System	
Sub3.3	Fiat Money Issuance and Sustained Expansion		Growth/stability	Borrowers, Asset holders	Savers, Fixed Income
	a. Reserves, reserves rates* policies (Re: IOER policy (2008))			Financial System	Currency holders
⓿	b. Special Case: Back-up financing (War, state finances; Re: moral hazard)		Security	Defense Industry	Currency holders
Sub3.4	Asset Purchases/Accumulation (Fiat Money-financed)		Growth/stability	Asset Sellers*	avers, Inc.-based paye
	*also see Sub3.2d loan guarantees, Sub1.4c bailouts/corp. welfare			*above markt value	
Sub3.5	Exchange Rate interventions *		Growth/stability		Currency holders
	a. currency depreciation/"beggar-thy-neighbor"			Export industry	Importers, consumers
	b. currency appreciation/overvalued currencies			Importers/consumers	Export industry
	*fiat money interventions in international currency markets			of imports/asset&financial	
Sub3.6	Fiat Money Policy, Extensions and Linkages				
	a. Demonetization as industrial policy		Growth/Stability	Tech, financial industry	Currency holders
*	b. Cryptocurrencies, alt-coins (leveraging of central bank fiat) *NON-POLICY		n/a or not stated		

SUBSYSTEM 3 of System 2

III. FIAT MONEY FINANCING/MONETARY POLICY—Cont' Phase 1 (Initial)

SUBSYSTEM 3 PHASES: Hypothesized elevated risk of occurrence (including delayed impacts)

Sub3.#	A. POLICY INTERVENTION TYPE	F. Rent-seeking activity	G. Impaired Production/Reduced Income Impacts	H. Shortages (incl. Food crises)	I. Black markets/violence due to contract non-legally	J. Clustering: Oversupply/ excess. Spec. and competition	K. Deficit/Debt (Expand-> Inflows) [Delay 1-Overshoot]	L. Secondary Policies/ Impacts (incl. extra-judicial/ state violence) [Delay 2-Reversal]	M. Ownership Insecurity (incl. self) hoarding	N. Visible protests/ unrest
Sub3.1	Reduction of Borrowing Costs (re: financial repression)	1								
	a. Interest Rate Decoupling (gap)					1c		Lowering of policy rates (negative)		
Sub3.2	Compensation to Financial Institutions					1c asset market bubbles		Bank reforms; capital requirements/stress testing		
	a. Lending cost reduction policy	1				1c high-yield speculation		Deposit insurance		
	b. Reserves Expansion Legality	1			1b					
	c. Caps on deposit rates	1		1a		1a		Crackdowns		
	d. Loan guarantees	1		1a loanable funds, 1b moneylenders						
Sub3.3	Fiat Money Issuance and Sustained Expansion	1				1c	1	Official controls	1*	1*
	a. Reserves, reserves rates* policies (Re: IOER policy (2008))					1c asset market bubbles or high-yield speculation		Vacant properties; short-sale curbs	*purchasin g power / *consumer price inflation	
⓿	b. Special Case: Back-up financing (War, state finances; Re: moral h	1						Extreme cases: Hyperinflations		
Sub3.4	Asset Purchases/Accumulation (Fiat Money-financed)	1					1	Pension, bank bailouts		
	*also see Sub3.2d loan guarantees; Sub3.4c bailouts/corp welfare									
Sub3.5	Exchange Rate Interventions *									
	a. currency depreciation/"beggar-thy-neighbor"	1		1d		1		Crackdowns		
	b. currency appreciation/overvalued currencies	1	1	1e	1	1	1	Crackdowns*	1	After removal
	*Fiat money interventions in international currency markets		1d. Imported goods, inputs	1e. Foreign currency				*currency speculators		
Sub3.6	Fiat Money Policy, Extensions and Linkages									
	a. Demonetization as industrial policy									
*	b. Cryptocurrencies, alt-coins (leveraging of central bank fiat) *NON-POLICY									

155

Conventions attempted in the book are mentioned here, although it is recognized that these conventions may not always be consistently applied. **Parentheses.** When a term appears in parentheses after another term [such as *creditors (lenders)*], the meaning of the two terms is taken to be very similar but possibly used in different contexts. The use of "i.e." within parentheses is designed to emphasize the term. "E.g." within parentheses is an abbreviation for "example" as in "for example." Also, "aka" is an abbreviation for "also known as"). Occasionally parentheses will be used in front of or behind another to mean that the word is optional but can help clarify the meaning. **"RE:" or "Re:"** is a *general* reference to an additional source of information related to the topic. Re: is often a concept or terminology, but can also be a work or author that may or may not appear in the *References* section and that should be searchable online. **Slashes**. Like parentheses, a slash (for example, debt/borrowings) means that both terms are nearly identical in meaning in that context and therefore "joined" together by a slash. **Italics** are added because of its deemed importance and often to indicate a technical or other terminology used in the field that could be researched elsewhere for background information. **Boldface** is intended usually to indicate a subtopic. **Currency Units** are at times stated (such as Dollars, Yuan, Euros, Yen) when necessary, but when a neutral example is provided that involves currency, the term "currency units" may also at times be used. **Quotation marks** are used either for emphatic effect, for a popularized term, informal jargon or common expression used in a field, industry, or context. **References** are from a wide variety of sources, academic, practitioner-oriented, and journalistic. It is recognized that using non-academic sources may appear to reduce the quality of the research, but this approach is considered preferable to identify variations in viewpoints--practitioners can offer valuable insights from their first-hand experiences in industry. Quality journalistic references can provide readers with more current information. References and citations do not necessarily imply agreement with, or endorsement of, the authors, whether individuals or related to a service or organization (e.g. a fund manager, group, political party, etc.). It can be difficult to cover certain topics without referring to possibly objectionable and unpopular research, ideas or individuals that might have fallen out of the mainstream; however, despite these concerns, it is hoped that drawing from diverse sources can help shed light on economic distortions and sustainable, just systems. If the same work is cited in succession, the same work may be indicated only by enclosing the page number in parentheses; it is assumed that the same work is being cited. Some citations are not direct and are sourced from another researcher. It is recognized that a citation may not be representative of, or fully convey, the entirety of a body of research and therefore can be misleading if not qualified. Citing a work doesn't imply approval of, or agreement with, the citation or the cited work or author(s). It is not unusual for some historical writings be confusing or inconsistent. It is understood that some educated guesswork may be necessary at times to ascertain what an author most likely intended to say, as even scholars in the field may be unable to fully agree on the meaning of certain passages.

REFERENCES

Alesina, Alberto and Giavazzi, Francesco (Eds.), *Fiscal policy after the Financial Crisis*, National Bureau of Economic Research (NBER), University of Chicago Press, 2013.

Anderson, T. W.; Darling, D. A. (1952). "Asymptotic theory of certain "goodness-of-fit" criteria based on stochastic processes". *Annals of Mathematical Statistics*. 23: 193–212.

Andrews, Dan., McGowan, Muge Adalet., and Millot, Valentine., "The Walking Dead? Zombie Firms and Productivity Performance in OECD Countries," *OECD Economics Department Working Papers* No. 1372, January 10, 2017.

Antonopoulos, Andreas M., *The Internet of Money*, (Vol 1, 2) Merkle Bloom LLC, 2016, 2017.

Bank for International Settlements (BIS), "Global Financial Markets Remain Dependent on Central Banks," Chapter II, *BIS 85th Annual Report 2014/15*, June 28, 2015, pp. 25-43.

Bank for International Settlements, "International Banking and Financial Market Developments", *BIS Quarterly Review*, Monetary and Economic Department, December 2017.

Barro, Robert J., "Are Government Bonds Net Wealth?", *Journal of Political Economy* (Vol. 82, no.6), University of Chicago, Nov/Dec 1974

BIS, see Bank for International Settlements.

Bohm-Bawerk, E. von., "The Function of Saving" *Annals of the American Academy of Political and Social Science* (May 1901).

Borio, C. and Disyatat, P.., " Low Interest Rates and Secular Stagnation: Is Debt a Missing Link?" *VOX*, June 2014.

Borio, Claudio., Erdem, Magdalena., Filardo, Andrew., Hofmann Boris., "The Cost of Deflations: A Historical Perspective," *BIS Quarterly Review*, March 2015.

Bowles, Samuel., Kirman, Alan., Sethi, Rajiv., "Retrospectives: Friedrich Hayek and the Market Algorithm," *Journal of Economic Perspectives* (Vol. 31 No. 3), Summer, 2017 (pp. 215-30).

Brainard, Lael., "Normalizing Monetary Policy When the Neutral Interest Rate Is Low," *Presentation at the Stanford Institute for Economic Policy Research*, Stanford, California, December 1, 2015.

Brealey, Richard A., and Myers, Stewart., *Principles of Corporate Finance*, The McGraw-Hill Companies, Inc., 1996.

Cantillon, Richard., *Essai sur la Nature du Commerce en Général (traduit de l'anglais)*, 1755.

Chakravarti, Laha, and Roy, (1967). *Handbook of Methods of Applied Statistics,* Volume I, John Wiley and Sons, pp. 392-394. (re: Kolmogorov-Smirnov)

Chi, Leisha., "Can Toshiba escape fate of corporate Japan's zombie hordes?" *BBC News Business*, April 16, 2017.

Christ, Carl., "A Simple Macroeconomic Model with a Government Budget Restraint," *Journal of Political Economy* 76 (1) (Jan/Feb 1968), 53-67.

Christ, Carl., "On Fiscal and Monetary Policies and the Government Budget Restraint," *The American Economic Review* 69(3-5) (1979), 526-538.

Cirillo, Pasquale., and Taleb, N.N., "On the Statistical Properties and Tail Risk of Violent Conflicts," Tail Risk Working Papers, *ArXiv*, Oct 19, 2015.

Cirillo, Pasquale., Fontanari, Andrea., and Taleb, Nassim, Nicholas., "Gini estimation under infinite variance,"; Risk Research Program, *ArXiv*, July 9, 2017.

Clarida, Richard., "Removing Accommodation" *PIMCO Global Central Bank Focus*, March 2017.

Clayton, Jay., "Statement on Cryptocurrencies and Initial Coin Offerings," *Public Statement*, U.S. Securities and Exchange Commission, December 11, 2017.

Cobb, C. W.; Douglas, P. H. (1928). "A Theory of Production". *American Economic Review* 18 (Supplement): 139–165.

Cohen, Jerome B. and Zinbarg, Edward D.., *Investment Analysis and Portfolio Management*, Richard D. Irwin, Inc., Homewood, Illinois 1967.

Cook, John. D., "Thick Tails," *John D. Cook Applied Mathematics Consulting* (johndcook.com), January 18, 2008.

Cook, John D., "Quantile-Quantile Plots and Powers of 3/2," *John D. Cook Applied Mathematics Consulting* (johndcook.com), April 2, 2017.

Coyne, Christopher and Coyne, Rachel (Eds.)., *Flaws and Ceilings: Price Controls and the Damage They Cause*, Institute of Economic Affairs, 2015.

Cramer, James J., *Real Money*, Simon & Schuster, 2009.

Damodaran, Aswath., *Investment Valuation*., John Wiley & Sons, Inc., 1996, (3rd Ed.) 2012.

De La Calle, L.S., (1544) *Instrucción de Mercaderes* ... (see Grice-Hutchinson 1952) (Re: *School of Salamanca*)

160

Devajaran, Shantayanan, and Anthony C. Fisher., "Hotelling's Economics of Exhaustible Resources: Fifty Years Later," *Journal of Economic Literature* Vol. XIX (March 1981), 65-73.

Dewing, Arthur Stone., *The Financial Policy of Corporations*, 5th Ed., The Ronald Press, 1953.

Dixon, Peter B. and Jorgenson, Dale., *Handbook of Computable General Equilibrium Modeling*, Volume 1A, Elsevier North Holland, 2013.

Dorsey, Pat., *The Five Rules for Successful Stock Investing: Morningstar's Guide to Building Wealth and Winning in the Market*, Morningstar, Inc., 1994.

Douady, R., and N.N. Taleb., "A Map and Simple Heuristic to Detect Fragility, Antifragility, and Model Error," *arXiv Preprint*, 2012.

El-Erian, Mohamed., *The Only Game in Town: Central Banks, Instability and Avoiding the Next Collapse*, Random House, New York, 2016.

Fabozzi, Frank J., The Handbook of *Fixed Income Securities, 8th Edition,* McGraw-Hill, 2011.

Fama, E.F. and French, K.R., "The Cross-Section of Expected Stock Returns," *Journal of Finance*, (47: 427-466), 1992.

Fama, E.F. and French, K.R., "The Capital Asset Pricing Model: Theory and Evidence," *Journal of Economic Perspectives* (Vol.18:3), 2004.

Fellman, Philip Vos., Bar-Yam, Yaneer, Minai, Ali A., Editors., *Conflict and Complexity*, Springer, 2016.

Ferguson, Niall., *The Great Degeneration*, Penguin Books, 2014.

Fetter, Frank A., "Interest Theories, Old and New," *The American Economic Review*, Volume IV, No. 1 (March 1914), 68-92.

Fisher, I., *The Theory of Interest (as Determined by Impatience to Spend Income and Opportunity to Invest It)*, New York: The Macmillan Company, 1930.

Forrester, Jay., "Counterintuitive Behavior of Social Systems," *Technology Review* 73 (3) 52-68, 1971. (Re: system dynamics)

Friedman, Milton., *Price Theory*, Walter de Gruyter: Aldine Publishing Company, 1986.

GAO (see General Accounting Office).

Gordon, M., *The Investment, Financing and Valuation of the Corporation*, Richard D. Irwin, Inc., Homewood, Illinois, 1962. (Re: Gordon Growth Model)

Gorroochum, Prakash., *Classic Topics on the History of Modern Mathematical Statistics*, John Wiley & Sons, 2016.

Graham, Benjamin., (1949) *The Intelligent Investor: The Classic Text on Value Investing*, Harper Business, 2005.

Grant, James., *Mr. Market Miscalculates: The Bubble Years and Beyond*, Axios Press, 2008.

Grant, James., *The Trouble with Prosperity*, Times Books/Random House, 1996.

Greenblatt, Joel., *The Little Book that Beats the Market*, John Wiley & Sons, 2006.

Grice-Hutchinson, M. (1952)., The *School of Salamanca: Readings in Spanish Monetary Theory, 1544-1605*, 1952. (also see Hutchison, Terence)

Gulbransen, Audun., "Money is a social construct and that's why you should run a #bitcoin full-node," *Medium,* November 2, 2017.

Gupta, Girish., "Venezuela money supply surges 10 percent in one week, fastest in 25 years," *Reuters*, July 29, 2017.

Hale, Thomas., "Pension Funds Turn to Mortgage Market in Search of Higher Yield, *Financial Times*, December 17, 2015.

Hanke, Steve H., "Venezuela: No Rule of Law, Bad Money," *Globe Asia*, May-June 2015 (reprinted: Cato Institute, Commentary).

Hanke, Steve H., "Venezuela's Grim Reaper -- A Weekly Report," *Zero Hedge*, August 29, 2017.

Hayek, Friedrich A., *Prices and Production,* London: Routledge, Kegan & Paul, 1931.

Hayek, Friedrich A., (1974), "The Pretense of Knowledge," essay presented at the occasion of Hayek's Nobel Prize in Economics, December 11, 1974, reprinted with permission by the Foundation for Economic Education (FEE).

Hayek, Friedrich A., "The Use of Knowledge in Society," *The American Economic Review*, Vol. 35, No. 4 (September 1945), pp. 519-530.

Heimann, Eduard., *History of Economic Doctrines*, Oxford University Press, 1964.

Hicks, J.R., *Value and Capital,* 2nd Ed., Clarendon Press, Oxford, 1946.

Hitchner, James R., *Financial Valuation: Applications and Models*, 3rd Ed., John Wiley & Sons, 2011.

Holland, Oscar., "Rare Da Vinci painting smashes world records with $450 million sale," *CNN*, November 16, 2017.

Hollingsworth, Barbara. "Economist Tells Congress: U.S. May Be in 'Worse Fiscal Shape' Than Greece," *CNS News*, March 9, 2015. (See Kotlikoff, 2015)

Holston, Kathryn., Laubach, Thomas., and Williams, John C., "Measures of the Natural Rate of Interest: International Trends and Determinants," *Federal Reserve Bank of San Francisco Working Paper Series*, Working Paper 2016-11, December 15, 2016.

Hotelling, Harold., "The Economics of Exhaustible Resources," *The Journal of Political Economy* 39 (2) (April 1931), 137-175.

Huerta de Soto, Jesus., *Money, Bank Credit, and Economic Cycles*, Ludwig von Mises Institute, 2012.

Hussman, John P., *Hussman Funds Weekly Market Comment*, "Estimating Market Losses at a Speculative Extreme," August 7, 2017; "Correlation of Various Valuation Measures with Actual Subsequent SPX Total Returns," September 23, 2017.

Hutchison, Terence., *Before Adam Smith: The Emergence of Political Economy*, 1662-1776, Basil Blackwell, Ltd., 1988.

Hutt, William., *A Rehabilitation of Say's Law*, Ohio University Press: Athens, 1974. (Also see Manhattan Institute, 1983)

International Monetary Fund, *"IMF World Economic Outlook (WEO)*, April 2015.

International Monetary Fund, "United States: Selected Issues Paper," *IMF Country Report* No. 10/248, July 2010.

Johnson N.I., "Systems of Frequency Curves Generated by Methods of Translation," *Biometrika* (36:149-176), 1949.

Juselius, M., Borio, C., Disyatat, P., and Drehmann, M., "Monetary Policy, the Financial Cycle and Ultra-Low Interest

Rates," *International Journal of Central Banking*, (13:3), 2017, pp 55-90.

Laplace, Pierre-Simon de., *Mémoire sur la Probabilité des Causes par les Evènements*, 1774. (see Gorroochum, 2016)

Laplace, Pierre-Simon de., *Mémoire sur les Probabilités*, 1781. (OC 9, Article XIII, p 477, 479; see Gorroochum 2016)

Laplace, Pierre-Simon de., *Mémoire sur les approximations des formules qui sont fonctions de très grands nombres (suite)*, 1786. (Article XXXII, OC10 pp 295-6; see Gorroochum 2016)

Liu, Sheen., and Wu, Chunchi., "Repo Counterparty Risk and On-/Off-the-Run Treasury Spreads," *The Review of Asset Pricing Studies*, Society for Financial Studies, Oxford University Press, (Vol. 7., Number 1), June 2017

Kennedy, Raoul., *Equity Income Analytics*, Amazon Publishing, LLC, 2014.

Kennedy, Raoul., *Interest Rate Analytics*, Amazon Publishing, LLC, 2015.

Kennedy, Raoul., *Rate-of-Return Analytics*, Amazon Publishing, LLC, 2016.

Kennedy, Raoul., *Economic Distortion Dynamics*, Amazon Publishing, LLC, 2017.

Keynes, John Maynard., *The General Theory of Employment, Interest, and Money,* London: Macmillan, 1936.

Klein, Lawrence R., *The Economics of Supply and Demand*, Basil Blackwell Publisher Limited, 1983.

Knight, Frank., (1921) *Risk, Uncertainty and Profit*, LSE reprints of scarce tracts, London, LSE [as cited in Backhouse (1987) and Friedman (1986)].

Kolmogorov, A. N., *Foundations of Probability* (*Grundbegriffe derWahrscheinlichkeitrechnung, Ergebnisse Der Mathematik*) translated as, New York: Chelsea Publishing Company, 1950.

Kolmogorov A (1933). "Sulla determinazione empirica di una legge di distribuzione". *G. Ist. Ital. Attuari*. 4: 83–91. (Re: K-S test statistic)

Kotlikoff, Lawrence J., "America's Fiscal Insolvency and Its Generational Consequences," *Testimony to the Senate Budget Committee*, 2015.

Krueger, Anne O., "The Political Economy of the Rent-Seeking Society," *American Economic Review* 64 (1974): 291-303. (*)

Kurzweil, Ray., "The Law of Accelerating Returns," (kurzweilai.net/the-law-of-accelerating-returns), March 7, 2001.

Kuznets, Simon., *Modern Economic Growth: Rate Structure and Spread*, New Haven, Yale University Press, 1966.

Laubach, Thomas, Williams., John C., "Measuring the Natural Rate of Interest Redux" *Federal Reserve Bank of San Francisco Working Paper Series 2015-16*, October 2015.

Laubach, Thomas, Williams, John C., "Measuring the Natural Rate of Interest," *Review of Economics and Statistics* (Vol 85, No. 4: 1063-1070) November 2003.

Leamer, E.E., "Let's Take the Con out of Econometrics," *American Economic Review*, 73 (1983), 31-43.

Lichtenfeld, Marc., *Get Rich with Dividends*, John Wiley & Sons, Inc., 2nd.Edition, 2015.

Lindahl, Erik., *Studies in the Theory of Money and Capital* (Translation: Tor Ferholm), London: Allen & Unwin, 1939.

Locke, John (1668) as cited in Hutchison (1988: 63). See Hutchison, Terence.

Locke, John (1689)., *Second Treatise on Government* (Chap. IV: 22), Hackett, 1980.

Lofchie, Michael., "Political and Economic Origins of African Hunger," *Journal of Modern African Studies*, Vol. 13:4, 1975: 551-67).

Lucas, Robert (1976). "Econometric Policy Evaluation: A Critique". In Brunner, K.; Meltzer, A. *The Phillips Curve and Labor Market*s. Carnegie-Rochester Conference Series on Public Policy 1. New York: American Elsevier. pp. 19–46.

Lundvall, Henrik., and Westermark, Andreas, "What is the Natural Interest Rate?" *Sveriges Riksbank Economic Review* (2011:2).

Malkiel, Burton., *A Random Walk Down Wall Street: The Time-Tested Strategy for Successful Investing*, (11th Edition), W.W. Norton & Company, 2016.

Malthus, Thomas. (1815), *An Inquiry into the Nature and Progress of Rent*, as cited in Winch (1987) Oxford University Press.

Manhattan Institute for Policy Research, "Hutt: An Economist for This Century", *Manhattan Report on Economic Policy*, Vol III No. 5., 1983.

Manrique, Marta., Marqués, José Manuel., "An Empirical Approximation of the Natural Rate of Interest and Potential Growth" *Documento de Trabajo No. 0416*, Banco de España, Madrid, 2004.

Markowitz, H.M., "Portfolio Selection," *The Journal of Finance* 7 (1): 77–91, March 1952.

Marx, Karl (1867)., *Capital: Volume 1: A Critique of Political Economy*, Penguin Classics; Reprint Edition (1992).

McCloskey, Dierdre N., "The Core of Liberty is Economic Liberty," *Foundation for Economic Education*, September 7, 2017.

McCormick, Liz., "Global Bond Rally Near 'Panic' Level with Japan Yield Below Zero," *Bloomberg Business*, Feb 9, 2016.

McCormick, Liz Capo, and Renick, Oliver., "Greenspan Warns of Bond Market Bubble," *Financial Advisor* (FA Online), August 1, 2017.

McKinnon, Ronald I., *Money & Capital in Economic Development,* Brooking Institution Press, 1973.

McKinsey Global Institute, "Debt and (Not Much) Deleveraging," *MGI Report*, McKinsey & Company, February 2015.

Miller, Merton H., and Charles W. Upton., "A Test of the Hotelling Valuation Principle," *Journal of Political Economy* 93 (1), 1985.

Mill, John Stuart (1848)., *Principles of Political Economy*, Books IV and V, Penguin Group, 1988. (Original 1848)

Mill, John Stuart (1859)., *On Liberty*, Dover Publications, 2002.

Mises, Ludwig von., (1912) *The Theory of Money and Credit* (translated from the German) 1934; also, Yale University Press, 1953.

Mises, Ludwig von., (1920) Economic *Calculation in the Socialist Commonwealth* (original: *"Die Wirtschaftrechnung im sozialistischen Gemeinwesen", Archiv fur Sozialwissenschaften* 47 (1920)), Ludwig von Mises Institute, 2012.

Mises, Richard von., *Probability and Statistics,* American Mathematical Society, 1964.

Mitchell, Daniel., (2017a) "Social Security's Creeping Fiscal Crisis," *International Liberty*, July 17, 2017.

Moody's Investors Service Global Credit Research, "Putting EBITDA in Perspective," *Special Comment*, June 2000.
Murray, Charles., *Coming Apart: The State of White America, 1960-2010*, Crown Forum, 2013.

Myint, H., *The Economics of the Developing Countries*, Hutchinson University Library, 1980.

Myrdal, Gunnar, *Monetary Equilibrium* (Translation: R.B. Bryce and N. Stolper), London: William Hodge & Company, 1939.

National Institute of Standards and Technology (NIST), Exploratory Data Analysis, EDA Techniques, Quantitative Techniques (1.3.5.14, 1.3.5.15, 1.3.5.16), *NIST/SEMATECH e-Handbook of Statistical Methods*, 2012. (*See references to goodness of fit testing)

Neumann, J.V., "A Model of General Economic Equilibrium," *The Review of Economic Studies*, Vol. 13 No.1 (1945-46), pp 1-9.

NIST, see National Institute of Standards and Technology.

OECD, *National Income Accounts at a Glance*, Organisation for Economic Cooperation, and Development, 2014.

Olofsson, Peter., *Probability, Statistics, and Stochastic Processes*, Wiley, 2011.

Organisation for Economic Cooperation and Development (see OECD).

Panico, Carlo., *Interest and Profit in the Theories of Value and Distribution*, The Macmillan Press, Ltd., 1988.

Paulos, John Allen., *Innumeracy*, Vintage Books, 1990.

169

Perry, Mark., "Don't Outlaw Price Gouging After Harvey. Let the Market Work," Opinion, *Newsweek*, August 28, 2017.

Peters, Josh., *The Ultimate Dividend Playbook*, Morningstar, Inc., 2008.

Peters, Josh., "Dividends, Cash and TINA," *Morningstar DividendInvestor,* Morningstar, Inc. (Vol. 12, No. 6), July 2016.

Piketty, Thomas., *Capitalism in the Twenty-First Century*, Harvard University Press, Cambridge, Mass., 2014.

Pindyck, Robert S., and Rubinfeld, Daniel L., *Econometric Models and Economic Forecasts*, McGraw-Hill International, 1991.

Pratt, Shannon P., *Valuing a Business*, 2nd Ed., Business One Irwin, 1989.

Rake, Alan., "The Collapse of African Agriculture," *African Development*, February 1975.

Reuters Staff, "Fitch: $9.7T of Negative Yielding Debt Despite Monetary Normalization, *Reuters*, December 11, 2017

Ricardo, David (1826)., (P. Sraffa, Ed. with M. Dobb)., *The Works and Correspondence of David Ricardo, Volume I: On the Principles of Political Economy and Taxation*, Cambridge: Cambridge University Press, 1951-1983.

Rickards, James., *The Death of Money: The Coming Collapse of the International Monetary System*, Portfolio, 2017.

Romer, David., "Dynamic Stochastic General Equilibrium Models of Fluctuations". *Advanced Macroeconomics* (Fourth ed.). New York: McGraw-Hill Irwin, pp. 312–364, 2012.

Ropke, Wilhelm., *Crises and Cycles* (adapted and revised by Vera C. Smith), William Hodge and Co. Ltd., 1936.

Rosenbaum, Joshua., Pearl, Joshua., *Investment Banking: Valuation, Leveraged Buyouts and Mergers & Acquisitions*, (2nd Ed.), 2013.

Ross, Stephen A., "The Arbitrage Theory of Capital Asset Pricing". *Journal of Economic Theory* 13 (3):341–360, 1976.

Ross, Stephen A., Westerfield, Randolph W., Jaffe, Jeffrey., *Corporate Finance*, 8th Ed., McGraw-Hill Irwin, 2008.

Rothbard, Murray., "Breaking out of the Walrasian Box: The Cases of Schumpeter and Hansen," *The Review of Austrian Economics*, Spring 1987, pp 97-108.

Rothbard, Murray., "Time Preference" in *Capital Theory* (John Eatwell, Murray Milgate, and Peter Newman, Eds.), W.W. Norton & Company, 1990.

Russo, Camila., "Ethereum Co-Founder Says Crypto Coin Market Is a Time Bomb," *Bloomberg Technology*, July 18, 2017.

Salerno, Joseph T., "The Fed and Bernanke Are Wrong About the Natural Interest Rate," *Mises Wire*, June 26, 2016.

Sandis, Constantin., and Taleb, Nassim., "The Skin in the Game Heuristic for Protection Against Tail Events," *ArXiv*, January 11, 2014 (v3).

Say, J.B., *Traité d'Economie Politique*, 1803.

Sayama, Hiroki., *Introduction to the Modeling and Analysis of Complex Systems*, Open SUNY Textbooks, Milne Library, 2015.

Schilt, James H., "A Rational Approach to Capitalization Rates for Discounting the Future Income Stream of Closely Held Companies, " *The Financial Planner*, Jan. 1982.

Schultz, Theodore W., (Ed) *Distortions of Agricultural Incentives*, Indiana University Press, 1978.

Serra, Antonio (1613*)., A Brief Treatise on the Causes which can make Gold and Silver Plentiful in Kingdoms where there are No Mines*, cited in Hutchison (1988) from Monroe A.E. (1924) *Early Economic Thought*.

Shedlock, Michael., "Zombie Corporations Litter Europe, Kept Alive by ECB," *Zero Hedge*, July 30, 2017 (originally published in MishTalk, July 29, 2017).

Shim, Jae K., Siegel, Joel G., and Simon, Abraham J., et al., *The Vest-Pocket MBA*, Prentice-Hall, Inc., 1986.

Shultz, Theodore W., *Distortions of Agricultural Incentives*, Bloomington, Indiana University Press, 1978.

Schumpeter, J.A. (1954)., *History of Economic Analysis,* Oxford University Press, 1996.

Sigurjónsson, Frosti., *Monetary Reform: A Better Monetary System for Iceland,* Reykjavik, Iceland, March 2015. (Report commissioned by the Prime Minister of Iceland, Edition 1.0, 2015).

Sironi, Paolo., *Fintech Innovation*, Wiley, 2016.

Smirnov N (1948). "Table for estimating the goodness of fit of empirical distributions". *Annals of Mathematical Statistics*. 19: 279–281. (Re: Table of K-S distribution)

Smith, Adam (1776), *An Inquiry into the Nature and Causes of the Wealth of Nations*, David Campbell Publishers Ltd., 1991 and University of Chicago Press, 1976.

Smithson, Michael., *Ignorance and Uncertainty: Emerging Paradigms*, Springer-Verlag 1989.

Snedecor, George W. and Cochran, William G., *Statistical Methods*, Eighth Edition, Iowa State University Press, 1989. (re: *Chi-Squared Test*)

Solow, Robert., "Building a Science of Economics for the Real World," *Prepared Statement of Robert Solow, Professor Emeritus, MIT, to the House Committee on Science and Technology, Subcommittee on Investigations and Oversight*, July 20, 2010.

Solzhenitsyn Aleksandr I., *The Gulag Archipelago* 1918-1956 I-II, Harper & Row; First Edition, 1973. (*)

Sowell, Thomas., *Say's Law*, Oxford University Press, 1973.

Sowell, Thomas., *A Conflict of Visions: Ideological Origins of Political Struggles*, Basic Books, 2007.

Spiegel, Murray R., Schiller, John., and Srinivasan, R. Alu., *Probability and Statistics*, 2nd Edition, Tata McGraw-Hill, 2006.

Spitznagel, Mark., "What Is This "Neutral" Interest Rate Touted by the Fed?", *Mises Wire*, January 3, 2017.

Spitznagel, Mark., "Why Cryptocurrencies Will Never Be Safe Havens," *Mises Wire*, August 14, 2017.

Stephens, M. A. (1974). "EDF Statistics for Goodness of Fit and Some Comparisons," *Journal of the American Statistical Association*, 69, pp. 730-737. (re: Anderson-Darling)

Stephens, M.A., (1986). "Tests Based on EDF Statistics". In D'Agostino, R. B.; Stephens, M. A. *Goodness-of-Fit Techniques*. New York: Marcel Dekker.

Stigler, George J., *The Theory of Price*, 4th Ed., Macmillan Publishing Co., 1987.

Stockman, David., *The Great Deformation: The Corruption of Capitalism in America*, PublicAffairs™, 2013.

Takeo, Yuko., Jeong Lee Ming., Hasegawa, Toshiro., "Japan's Central Bank is Distorting the Market, Bourse Chief Says," *Bloomberg*, July 20, 2017.

Taleb, Nassim Nicholas., *The Black Swan*, Random House Trade Paperbacks, 2010.

Taleb, Nassim Nicholas., *Antifragile: Things That Gain from Disorder*, Random House, 2012.

Taleb, Nassim Nicholas., (2016b) "Inequality and Skin in the Game," *Medium*, December 28, 2016.

Taleb, Nassim Nicholas., "Stochastic Tail Exponent for Asymmetric Power Laws," *arXiv.org Quantitative Finance*, Cornell University Library, April 5, 2017.

Tapscott, Don., and Tapscott, Alex., *Blockchain Revolution*, Portfolio/Penguin, 2016.

Theil, Peter., *Zero to One: Notes on Startups, or How to Build the Future*, Crown Business, 2014.

Trautwein, Hans-Michael., "Interest, Neutral Rate of," *International Encyclopedia of the Social Sciences*, Thomson Gale, 2008.

Tullock, Gordon., "The Welfare Costs of Tariffs, Monopolies and Theft," *Western Economic Journal* 5 (1967): 224-232. (*)

Tullock, Gordon., *Rent Seeking*, Edward Elgar, 1993. (*)

Von Mises (Ludwig, Richard), von Hayek., see Mises, Hayek.

Walker, Francis A., *Political Economy*, Henry Holt and Company, New York, 1888.

Weil, David., *Economic Growth*, (2nd Ed.), Prentice Hall, 2008

White, Lawrence., "Antifragile Banking and Monetary Systems," *Cato Journal*, Vol. 33, No. 3 (Fall 2013), 471-484.

Wickens, Michael., *Macroeconomic Theory: A Dynamic General Equilibrium Approach*, Second Edition, Princeton University Press, 2011.

Wicksell, Knut., *Geldzins und Guterpreise*, (Interest and Prices) Jena, 1898 (English-language translations 1936, 1965: Interest and Prices, New York, Kelley 1965).

Additional Notes, Resources, and Acknowledgements
Some references may not have been cited but may have some tangential relevance to the topics covered or the other references, particularly historical documents. Other references are included because they were omitted from previous works and a record of them is desired; these are marked with an asterisk. Interest rate data were sourced from the Board of Governors of the Federal Reserve System (US) online databases. Annual financial statements of firms are sourced from the filings with the U.S. Securities and Exchange Commission (SEC) or from company annual reports containing financial statements. Other resources include the NASDAQ, *Wikipedia, Wikimedia Commons, MathWave, Wikinvest, Econ Library* (econlib.org; David R. Henderson), *Investing* dot com, *Seeking Alpha* and contributors focused on dividend investing (e.g. David Fish) and *Yahoo Finance*. Special thanks to the Taipei Institute of Banking and Finance.